BAAC

The Discussion Book

The Discussion Book

50 Great Ways to Get People Talking

Stephen D. Brookfield
and Stephen Preskill

JB JOSSEY-BASS™
A Wiley Brand

Copyright © 2016 by John Wiley & Sons, Inc. All rights reserved.

Published by Jossey-Bass
A Wiley Brand
One Montgomery Street, Suite 1000, San Francisco, CA 94104-4594—www.josseybass.com

No part of this publication may be reproduced, stored in a retrieval system, or transmitted in any form or by any means, electronic, mechanical, photocopying, recording, scanning, or otherwise, except as permitted under Section 107 or 108 of the 1976 United States Copyright Act, without either the prior written permission of the publisher, or authorization through payment of the appropriate per-copy fee to the Copyright Clearance Center, Inc., 222 Rosewood Drive, Danvers, MA 01923, 978-750-8400, fax 978-646-8600, or on the Web at www.copyright.com. Requests to the publisher for permission should be addressed to the Permissions Department, John Wiley & Sons, Inc., 111 River Street, Hoboken, NJ 07030, 201-748-6011, fax 201-748-6008, or online at www.wiley.com/go/permissions.

Limit of Liability/Disclaimer of Warranty: While the publisher and author have used their best efforts in preparing this book, they make no representations or warranties with respect to the accuracy or completeness of the contents of this book and specifically disclaim any implied warranties of merchantability or fitness for a particular purpose. No warranty may be created or extended by sales representatives or written sales materials. The advice and strategies contained herein may not be suitable for your situation. You should consult with a professional where appropriate. Neither the publisher nor author shall be liable for any loss of profit or any other commercial damages, including but not limited to special, incidental, consequential, or other damages. Readers should be aware that Internet Web sites offered as citations and/or sources for further information may have changed or disappeared between the time this was written and when it is read.

Jossey-Bass books and products are available through most bookstores. To contact Jossey-Bass directly call our Customer Care Department within the U.S. at 800-956-7739, outside the U.S. at 317-572-3986, or fax 317-572-4002.

Wiley publishes in a variety of print and electronic formats and by print-on-demand. Some material included with standard print versions of this book may not be included in e-books or in print-on-demand. If this book refers to media such as a CD or DVD that is not included in the version you purchased, you may download this material at http://booksupport.wiley.com. For more information about Wiley products, visit www.wiley.com.

Library of Congress Cataloging-in-Publication Data is Available:

ISBN 978-1-119-04971-5 (paper)
ISBN 978-1-119-05091-9 (ePDF)
ISBN 978-1-119-05096-4 (ePUB)

Cover design by Wiley

Printed in the United States of America
FIRST EDITION

PB Printing   10 9 8 7 6 5 4

CONTENTS

PREFACE

This is a short book so this will be a short preface.

The two of us have long wanted a brief and accessible book—a manual, really—that collected the best techniques to start discussion, keep it going, and stay focused. This would be the kind of book you could stuff into a pocket or purse as you walked to chair a meeting, teach a class, or run a professional development workshop. On the way you could scan it to get a couple of new techniques to try out that day. To paraphrase *Dragnet's* Joe Friday, we wanted a manual containing "just the facts ma'am" or, rather, just the techniques.

AUDIENCE

Our audience for this book is probably the largest one either of us has ever written for. Essentially we hope that anyone who uses some kind of group discussion process in any setting at all will find it valuable. The convener of a corporate decision-making meeting or the leader of a community town hall or congregation will find this just as beneficial as will a classroom teacher.

We have tried out these techniques in an incredible variety of settings. In addition to the hundreds of schools and colleges we have worked with, these have been used in places as varied as the Occupy movement, corporations (including IBM, 3M, CA

Technologies, ARCO Oil), post–Hurricane Sandy community groups, the military, health care organizations, churches, and nonprofit organizations such as the Theater Development Fund in New York. Educational institutions using them have been as diverse as fashion institutes, schools of mining, chiropractic and Asian medicine colleges, schools for the deaf, seminaries, tribal colleges, and, of course, multiple two- and four-year colleges and universities.

So, if you're looking for some quick and easy techniques to try out in your meetings, workshops, or classrooms that will get people participating, focus the conversation, and keep the energy level high, then this is the book for you!

OVERVIEW OF CONTENTS

This book doesn't have traditional chapters, just a listing of fifty techniques we find applicable for multiple purposes in multiple settings, We imagine readers approaching a meeting, class, or workshop thinking, "I need to get more discussion going today," "as a group we need to listen better to what each other is saying," or "how am I going to democratize the session today so more people participate?"

We created a brief user guide to the book that identifies ten categories, each of which identifies a particular purpose the techniques are suited to. If this is your first time working with a group, you'd go to the first category on getting discussions going and consider trying something from there. If you feel that a few people are dominating the conversation then you'd consult the category on democratizing participation and select one of the ten techniques listed.

This means you as a reader don't need to look through a list of fifty techniques and pick one that fits. And you don't need to go through this book sequentially. Instead you can start with whichever of the following categories that seem to address your situation the best and see if any of the techniques listed there could work with your group.

· Top Ten Techniques to Get Discussion Going with New Groups
· Top Ten Techniques to Promote Good Questioning
· Top Ten Techniques to Foster Active Listening
· Top Ten Techniques for Holding Discussions without Speech
· Top Ten Techniques to Get People out of their Comfort Zone
· Top Ten Techniques for Text-Based Discussions
· Top Ten Techniques to Democratize Participation
· Top Ten Techniques to Transition from Small to Large Groups
· Top Ten Techniques for Building Group Cohesion
· Top Ten Techniques for Discussions Requiring a Decision

Because many of the techniques we use show up in multiple categories, we end with a list of the Top Ten Techniques That Best Serve Multiple Discussion Purposes.

WEBSITE

As an accompaniment to the book we have created a website devoted to it: www.thediscussionbook.com/. There you can find out how to contact us, reviews and applications of the techniques we've used, and examples of other techniques we couldn't fit into a short manual.

USER GUIDE

Top Ten Techniques to Get Discussion Going with New Groups

- Circle of Voices
- Chalk Talk
- Participation Rubric
- Think-Pair-Share
- Today's Meet
- Appreciative Pause
- Single Word Sum-Ups
- Setting Ground Rules
- The Three-Person Rule
- Quick Writes

Top Ten Techniques to Promote Good Questioning

- Strategic Questioning
- Open-ended Questions
- Nominating Questions
- If You Could Only Ask One Question
- On-the-Spot Questions
- What Do *You* Think?
- Clearness Committee

- Team Modeling
- Question Brainstorm
- Narrative Listening and Questioning

Top Ten Techniques to Foster Active Listening

- Circular Response
- Critical Conversation Protocol
- What Are You Hearing?
- Understanding Check
- Stand Where You Stand
- Clearness Committee
- Team Modeling
- Circle of Voices
- Narrative Listening and Questioning
- Single Word Sum-Ups

Top Ten Techniques for Holding Discussions without Speech

- Newsprint Dialogue
- Drawing Discussion
- Musicalizing Discussion
- Structured Silence
- Writing Discussion
- Appreciative Pause–Sticky Note Plaudit
- Critical Incident Questionnaire (CIQ)
- Chalk Talk
- Today's Meet
- Quick Writes

Top Ten Techniques to Get People out of Their Comfort Zone

- Methodological Belief
- Justifiable Pressure
- Cocktail Party
- Dramatizing Discussion
- Musicalizing Discussion
- Drawing Discussion
- Stand Where You Stand
- Clearness Committee
- Chalk Talk
- Today's Meet

Top Ten Techniques for Text-Based Discussions

- Hatful of Quotes
- Quotes to Affirm and Challenge
- Jigsaw
- Titling the Text
- Critical Debate
- Deliberative Polling
- Stand Where You Stand
- If You Could Only Ask One Question
- Question Brainstorm
- Quick Writes

Top Ten Techniques to Democratize Participation

- Common Ground
- Deliberative Polling
- Participatory Decision Making

- Circle of Voices
- Chalk Talk
- Critical Incident Questionnaire (CIQ)
- Newsprint Dialogue
- Circular Response
- Nominating Questions
- Today's Meet

Top Ten Techniques to Transition from Small to Large Groups

- Rotating Stations
- Snowballing
- Canvassing for Common Ground
- Newsprint Dialogue
- Drawing Discussion
- Musicalizing Discussion
- Dramatizing Discussion
- Stand Where You Stand
- Nominating Questions
- Critical Incident Questionnaire (CIQ)

Top Ten Techniques for Building Group Cohesion

- Mutual Invitation
- Understanding Check
- Circular Response
- Critical Incident Questionnaire
- Narrative Listening and Questioning
- Jigsaw
- Appreciative Pause–Sticky Note Plaudit

- Clearness Committee
- Common Ground
- Participatory Decision Making

Top Ten Techniques for Discussions Requiring a Decision

- Deliberative Polling
- Participatory Decision Making
- Canvassing for Common Ground
- Clearness Committee
- Critical Incident Questionnaire (CIQ)
- Nominating Questions
- Titling the Text
- Jigsaw
- Critical Conversation Protocol
- What Do *You* Think?

Top Ten Techniques That Best Serve Multiple Discussion Purposes

- Conversational Moves
- Conversational Roles
- Facilitator Summation
- Circle of Voices
- Participation Rubric
- Team Modeling
- Setting Ground Rules
- Today's Meet
- Chalk Talk
- Critical Conversation Protocol

ACKNOWLEDGMENTS

Stephen Brookfield would like to acknowledge his colleague, friend, and coauthor, Steve Preskill. Steve suggested the book, provided the passion that fueled it, and was a consistently creative, energetic, and funny partner. The two of us have worked on three books together now and all have been a delight. To have a best friend be a professional collaborator is a rare gift and one for which Stephen is eternally grateful.

Stephen Preskill would like to acknowledge Stephen Brookfield for agreeing to write another book with him and for more than twenty years of warm friendship and productive collaborations. Stephen has been an unending source of humor, good fun, and creative energy. And with Stephen's support and mentorship, Steve has not only become a much better writer and teacher, he has become a better person as well.

Both of us would like to thank all the community members, workshop participants, colleagues, and students who have told us over the years, "I tried that out and here's how it worked." You helped us hone and refine these techniques to serve a wide audience.

THE AUTHORS

Stephen D. Brookfield has written, coauthored, and edited seventeen books on adult learning, teaching, and critical thinking, six of which have won the Cyril O. Houle World Award for Literature in Adult Education (in 1986, 1989, 1996, 2005, 2011, and 2012). He also won the 1986 Imogene Okes Award for Outstanding Research in Adult Education and the 2013 Phillip E. Frandson Award for Outstanding Literature in Continuing Education. His work has been translated into German, Finnish, Korean, Japanese, Polish, and Chinese. He has been awarded three honorary doctor of letters degrees from the University System of New Hampshire (1991), Concordia University (2003), and Muhlenberg College (2010) for his contributions to understanding adult learning and shaping adult education. In 2001 he received the Leadership Award from the Association for Continuing Higher Education (ACHE) for "extraordinary contributions to the general field of continuing education on a national and international level." He currently serves on the editorial boards of educational journals in Britain, Canada, Italy, and Australia, as well as in the United States. During 2002 he was a visiting professor at Harvard University. After a decade as professor of higher and adult education at Columbia University in New York City, he has spent the last twenty years at the University of St. Thomas in Minneapolis, Minnesota, where he holds the title of the John Ireland Endowed Chair. In 2008 he won the university's Diversity in Teaching and Research Award and the John Ireland Teaching and Scholarship Award. In 2008 he was also awarded the Morris T. Keeton Award from the Council on Adult and Experiential Learning. In 2009 he was inducted into the International Adult Education Hall of Fame.

Stephen Preskill was most recently named professor emeritus at Wagner College in Staten Island, New York. Previously, he was Distinguished Professor of Civic Engagement and Leadership in Wagner College's Center for Leadership and Engagement, where he helped to advance Wagner's commitment to community-engaged teaching and scholarship and played a significant role in supporting student participation in community-based activism and leadership development. He is the coauthor of three books: *Stories of Teaching* (2001), *Discussion as a Way of Teaching* (2nd ed.) (2005), and *Learning as a Way of Leading* (2009), as well as the author of numerous articles, book reviews, and op-ed pieces. He is passionate about democracy and its potential to transform colleges and communities. He has a BA in history from Ithaca College, masters' degrees in history and education from Long Island University and special education from the University of Vermont, and a PhD in educational policy studies from the University of Illinois at Urbana-Champaign.

The Discussion Book

INTRODUCTION

You all know the scene. Another day, another meeting, and a feeling of complete pointlessness descending on you as you make your way to the conference room. Or you trudge to a mandatory leadership, staff, or professional development workshop expecting to be alternately bored and chastised while an "expert" tells you how you can be a better teacher, leader, decision maker, team member; how you can think out of the box, incorporate technology, address diversity, and generally be a pedagogic superhero. Alternatively you plod to class knowing that your efforts to get students to discuss the assigned reading will be met by awkward silence, averted eyes, and a reluctance to talk that swirls in the classroom atmosphere like a thick, Victorian London fog.

If you're a participant in a mandatory training workshop or departmental meeting you ask yourself, "Is there any way I can surreptitiously get some useful work done while this charade is happening?" When the leader or chair opens the session by saying he welcomes all questions and that nothing is off the table you think, "Yeah, right, how many times have I heard *that* before?" We have all endured counterfeit meetings and discussions: those that look as though some form of democratic group decision-making process is happening but in which the currency on offer—people engaged in apparently open-ended talk—is a forgery. It's counterfeit because although it looks like a genuine consideration of alternatives is happening, everyone knows the major decisions lie outside the room. And, although it seems superficially as if people are interested in, and eager to hear, what others have to say, you know this is really a sophisticated form of organizational playacting. You do it because this is what good teamwork is supposed to look like. But take it seriously? No way.

If you're running the event, it's even more stressful. You enter the room expecting a mix of apathy and resistance. If it's a class, you're betting that the students won't have done the prereading that's been assigned to inform the upcoming discussion and that getting people to speak will be like drawing blood from the proverbial stone. If it's a meeting, you know that the usual egomaniacs will dominate, often blocking any new initiatives you propose. If it's professional development training, you know there will be clumps of resisters with their arms folded and locked high across their chest. Their body language screams, "Motivate me to find this interesting, I dare you!"

People are bored and burned with group routine. We have all sat through so many lifeless classes, meetings, and PowerPoint-dominated trainings that it's no surprise that we have become skeptical or cynical. As a bumper sticker we saw once said, "no one dies wishing they had gone to more meetings."

But this doesn't have to be the case. The truth is that bad group deliberation usually happens because no protocols or exercises are used that involve everyone and that use multiple forms of engagement. In *The Discussion Book* we provide our top fifty strategies that get people talking in a purposeful and energized way. From urban high schools to Ivy League doctoral education programs, corporations to the military, international development agencies to social movements, and community groups to health care organizations, we have found that what people say they want is very consistent. They ask for very practical techniques to help them do the following:

- Get students, employees, reports to, colleagues, and citizens to participate more fully in group deliberation and decision making
- Provide new ways of running groups so participants feel more energized and engaged
- Encourage groups to keep focused on important topics, contentious issues, and key questions instead of getting diverted into trivia or avoidance
- Spur creativity so that people are actively asking unusual questions, uncovering new perspectives, and proposing novel solutions
- Increase genuine collaboration and teamwork, right from the outset of a group's time together

These goals are not easily achieved. But they will hardly *ever* be realized if you rely on the mystery of group chemistry. The keys to activating purposeful, productive, and participatory discussions are actually very simple. In every institution, organization, or community we have worked, good, engrossing talk only happens if the following conditions are in place:

- Protocols used are designed to equalize participation, keep people focused, and encourage new questions and perspectives.
- A variety of deliberative and decision-making formats ensure that people don't lose energy by falling into typical routines

· The leader, consultant, or trainer models her or his commitment to the protocols they ask others to engage in.

THE ZEN OF PROTOCOLS—YOU HAVE TO PLAN FOR SPONTANEITY

We both used to have faith in spontaneous group process. Early on in our careers we thought that whether or not groups worked well was essentially inscrutable. If the right people came together there would be a joyful combustion of energetic brainstorming with everyone involved. We're not saying that this never happens, but it's the Bigfoot of classroom, organizational, and community life—secretive, rarely seen.

However, there are things you can do to ensure that groups work well. You have to make sure everyone gets a chance to participate and that no one dominates by force of personality or organizational rank. You have to find ways of discussing problems and developing solutions that accommodate the different ways people process information and communicate with each other—visual, graphic, and kinetic, as well as through speech. Quieter, more introverted members need to feel there is time to formulate their contributions. Pretty much all the protocols we propose in this book are designed to elicit maximum participation from all involved.

Groups will also inevitably stray off topic as people become fixated on how an issue, topic, proposed change, or problem affects their little corner of the world. They want to follow their agenda or interest, even when it doesn't connect with what is being talked about, so you have to find ways of keeping the group focused while not losing the value of an unexpected idea or insight. It's a tough balance, but you have little hope of striking it unless you introduce protocols to help a class, meeting, case conference, or training refocus. That's a second intent built into most of our fifty techniques.

One of the hardest things to do is to keep people fresh and open so that a new way of looking at an old topic, issue, or problem can pop into their head. Some of the best sessions we've been involved in where those when someone said something like "you know maybe A is not the real problem. Perhaps what's really behind this is B." Problems can be recast spontaneously when a light bulb goes off in someone's head. It's making it a daily element of classroom, organizational, and community life that's the trick.

Protocols that institutionalize this behavior can be enormously helpful, particularly if the teacher, leader, trainer, department head, or consultant models his or her own engagement in this. Much of this boils down to the art of asking good questions, so embedded in many of our protocols is guidance on what good questions look like. Of course we have to model our own attempt to do this, something we'll say a little more about in a moment.

SPICING IT UP—AN ENERGETIC BLEND

Even the most energizing discussion protocol becomes routine if it's overused. You need to make people feel that they're not quite sure what's going to happen in the class, meeting, or training today. It's a kind of pleasurable uncertainty. Being surprised is one of the joys in life, and if that's built into how you convene people to talk with each other then you have far more chance of keeping them engaged.

No one technique will do all the things we want. There is no Holy Grail of group process. And if someone tries to convince you that they have it, you can be pretty sure they haven't done much facilitation and can promise you a steal of a deal on the Golden Gate Bridge.

Variety is the spice of life. The way to keep group gatherings spicy is to have lots of flavors in your spice rack of protocols. A pinch of *Chalk Talk* today, a soupcon of *Methodological Belief* tomorrow keeps the pot boiling pleasurably. The fifty techniques in this book are the top fifty we use most frequently, but we have a lot more and we're constantly developing new ones. You'll find these on the website we developed to accompany this book: www.thediscussionbook.com/. If you conduct weekly classes, trainings, or meetings, then, counting out holidays, this book provides a new protocol to try every week of the year!

MODELING YOUR COMMITMENT—WALKING THE TALK

Nothing produces cynicism quicker than the message, "Do as I say, not as I do." This is the basis of counterfeit democracy and counterfeit discussion. One of us was once part of a task force examining ways to think critically about every aspect of organizational life—except the office of the CEO. A sure recipe to guarantee no one took our report seriously.

In our experience all kinds of leaders are also victims of the myth of innocence. This myth assumes that if your intentions are pure, people will somehow mysteriously breathe in this purity and know that everything you do is in their best interest. It's leadership by osmosis.

But leadership by example is what everyone, including the two of us, craves. The most common criticism we hear of teachers, leaders, and supervisors boils down to "he doesn't walk the talk" or "she doesn't practice what she preaches." So if you use group protocols you need to show you take them seriously enough to engage in them yourself. For example, before asking people to practice these techniques the two of us always try to demonstrate how we do them with each other, perhaps using a topic or question suggested by a participant. Whenever possible we also participate in any exercise we have assigned.

It's important to model commitment, not perfection. Your intent is to show how you strive to implement a protocol, not to demonstrate it flawlessly. When we model a technique we take frequent pauses, talk about how hard it is to do well, and admit when we're struggling. Of course, we also own up to times when something is working really well for us. Our conviction is that we have no right to ask anyone else to try something out until we've done it first.

TO THE TECHNIQUES!

We present each of our techniques in a particular format. We begin with a statement of the purposes the technique is intended to accomplish followed by a clear and concrete description of the technique and how it's implemented. Then we report where and when each technique works well and what users say they like most about it. Next we alert readers to potential difficulties we have noticed when using the technique. We finish, when appropriate, with sample questions we have posed to groups.

A final comment. People often contact us asking for permission to use a technique we've written about. Please know there's no need to do this: we grant you permission to use anything you find in this book that you think might be useful. We urge you to steal from the book!

You can also change any technique in any way you want. Delete things, add things, blend elements of different techniques together, change how you implement them; do these all with our blessing. And we'd love it if you'd let us know about your experience trying out anything you find in the pages ahead. You can contact us at sdbrookfield@stthomas.edu or spreskill@gmail.com.

CHAPTER 1

Circle of Voices

Circle of Voices is a small-group exercise (four to six members) designed to secure early participation of all participants in a class, meeting, staff development training, workshop, or any other group event.

PURPOSES
· To create an early opportunity for everyone to participate
· To make sure the widest possible range of views are heard early on
· To prevent a premature consensus or focus emerging
· To socialize people into the habit of actively listening to others' contributions
· To stop the most extroverted or domineering from having undue influence

HOW IT WORKS

- Start by posing a question, issue, or problem to the group.
- Give everyone two minutes to think quietly about his or her responses. Stress that this phase is silent and make sure this is observed. Tell people to jot down notes summarizing their thoughts.
- When the two minutes are up ask people to form into groups of five.
- Each person in the group takes a turn to present his or her initial response to the question, issue, or problem posed. They are asked to keep their response to a minute—which usually means each person takes more like two!
- As each person gives a response there are to be no interruptions, not even supportive statements such as, "Yes, I've found that's true" or "You hit the nail on the head." These are in effect five or six brief monologues.
- Once the initial round of individual responses is over the group moves into the second round of conversation that is open and relatively unstructured. There is no order that needs to be followed. People contribute whenever they wish.
- In this second round, however, a ground rule comes into play about the kind of contributions people can make. People are allowed to talk only about what another person said in the first round. This can include asking questions about someone's initial contribution, commenting on something that resonated, disagreeing with a comment, or indicating how a first-round contribution opened up a new line of thinking.
- The exercise ends with people reporting (1) any new perspectives or resolutions they heard and (2) any new questions that were raised.

WHERE AND WHEN IT WORKS WELL

In the early stages of a class, meeting, training, or workshop. We usually do this in the first and second meetings in a series of group events.

With groups unused to discussion process. We have used this with freshman students in college, newly convened community groups, adults returning to higher education, and organizational members used to rigid meeting protocols.

WHAT USERS APPRECIATE

The initial two-minute silent pause for thinking. Introverts, second-language speakers, and reflectively oriented group members feel comfortable because they have time to think through their response and make notes to guide their contribution.

It gives everyone in the room the opportunity to be heard from. People appreciate the contributions and insights from people who don't usually speak up.

It emphasizes respectful listening. The second ground rule forces people to pay close attention to what other members are saying.

WHAT TO WATCH OUT FOR

Participants ignoring the time. Despite the instruction for people to take only about a minute to give their initial response in the opening round, some people are congenitally unable to do this. When you're chairing a meeting you can deal with this relatively easily by indicating (verbally or with gestures such as a time-out signal) that it's time to end the discussion of a particular item.

If you're teaching a class, running a professional development workshop, or hosting a community forum, you need to survey the room and watch for anyone who is clearly talking for too long or interrupting. When this happens, go over to the group and say, "time to move on to another contribution," "let's hear from the next person," or "remember, only one minute."

Ignoring the second-round ground rule. The first time they try *Circle of Voices* people often get to the open discussion and forget to focus only on what others said in the first round. If you're sitting in a group you can correct this, but when multiple groups are talking you can't check on them all. However, if this dynamic happens participants will most likely record that on the *Critical Incident Questionnaire (CIQ)* (technique 10) and you can address it with the group the next time it meets.

QUESTIONS SUITED TO THIS TECHNIQUE

We like this exercise because it can accommodate so many different kinds of questions. We tend to use it at the beginning of a workshop, course, or series of meetings.

· When for the best use of time: "What do we most need to consider today?"
· To identify agenda items: "What problem has taken up most of your time during the last week?"
· As stocktaking questions: "What's gone well for you since we met?"
· For questions of application: "What's an example of the theory we discussed?"
· To assess understanding: "Why is hypothesis A plausible?" "What's the most important point made in the prereading for today?"

CHAPTER 2

Chalk Talk

Developed by Hilton Smith (2009) of the Foxfire Fund, this is a great way to get a quick visual and graphic representation of where a group is on an issue. It's very brief—no more than five minutes long—and done in silence. *Chalk Talk* is a good way to unearth the concerns of a wide range of organizational members before building agendas for change or to discover how well students understand an issue or topic.

PURPOSES

- To produce a graphic representation of where a group, team, or class stands on an issue or topic in a way that indicates points of shared agreement, clusters of different or opposing viewpoints, and outlier perspectives to be considered

- To secure at least 60 percent participation (it's often much higher), which, in our experience, *Chalk Talk* invariably accomplishes
- To accommodate those in a group who process information and express themselves visually and graphically
- To allow introverts, second-language speakers, and reflectively oriented group members to feel comfortable about taking time to contribute something

HOW IT WORKS

- The leader writes a question in the center of a black or white board (or electronically) and circles it. In auditoriums or large staff development trainings we have sometimes had to cover several walls with blank sheets of newsprint for groups to write on. Markers or chalk sticks are placed by the board.
- Everyone is invited to come and stand by the board to participate in the activity. The leader explains that for about five minutes people should write responses to the question on the board. She also asks for silence for the next few minutes.
- Several people usually get up immediately and start writing simultaneously on different parts of the board. There are frequent pauses between postings.
- Those who are not writing at any point are asked to draw lines between comments that connect in some way. If they have questions or responses to a posting they also write that on the board.
- The facilitator also participates by drawing lines connecting comments, writing questions, adding her own thoughts, and so on.

- The facilitator closes the silent part of the exercise when the board is so full that posting new comments is difficult or when there's a distinct lull in posting.
- The facilitator and the group then talk about the graphic that has been produced. They identify clusters of common responses, questions that have been raised, and different analytical perspectives. Outlier comments are also noted.
- The leader invites people to take out smartphones, tablets, and laptops to snap photos of the *Chalk Talk* board and volunteers to post these to a group website.
- If this exercise is used in an organizational setting the group then identifies issues emerging from *Chalk Talk* that will be addressed by teams that people volunteer for. These teams then develop these issues into new organizational agendas.
- If this exercise is used in an academic class to introduce a new topic, the instructor alerts students to the plan to return regularly to themes and questions noted in the graphic.

WHERE AND WHEN IT WORKS WELL

This is very adaptable, and we've used it hundreds of times in a wide range of academic classrooms, professional development activities, staff training, and community meetings. It seems to work best in these settings:

At the outset of a series of meetings or classes. It lets group members see the range of different ways a topic, problem, or question can be understood or addressed.

Where you need the big picture. This is a good way to produce a global big picture of multiple perspectives and different solutions to problems. It stops a group from prematurely zeroing in on the most obvious solution.

To summarize what a group has learned or come to understand better. *Chalk Talk* can be used as a stocktaking evaluation of a long-term project or at the end of a course unit.

With a group composed of people from different organizational units and disciplinary backgrounds. It shows people that others who work and live close by don't always see things in the same way. The lines connecting points on different parts of the board also indicate similar concerns and points of possible agreement.

WHAT USERS APPRECIATE

Its visual nature. It's refreshing for graphically inclined learners to move away from speech and present something pictorially.

The time to process. Although the exercise time is brief there seems to be more time to think and process before posting a comment or drawing a connecting line.

How participatory it is. It gets a high percentage of people involved.

The extraverts can't dominate. No one's posting can be louder or more dominant than anybody else's.

The visual record it creates. The final graphic can be referred back to in subsequent meetings, workshops, and classes.

WHAT TO WATCH OUT FOR

Keeping the group size manageable. Up to twenty participants probably can do this easily. If the group is larger, there are problems seeing the board and getting there to post something.

In large auditoriums, we typically create four or five temporary white boards using newsprint sheets and ask people to move to the one closest to them. The downside is that debriefing each group's work adds time to the exercise.

People talking. For extraverts five minutes is a long time to remain silent. Inevitably some start to engage in side conversations or address the whole group, and you have to remind them that this exercise should be silent.

Nonparticipants. There is usually a group of nonparticipants who refuse to get out of their seats. All you can do is go over and invite them to move to the board.

QUESTIONS MOST SUITED TO THIS TECHNIQUE

- Questions to demonstrate diversity: "What does good practice look, sound, or feel like?"
- Questions to assess understanding: "What is a proof?"
- Questions to introduce a topic: "What do we need to know about photosynthesis?" "When have you witnessed or enacted a micro-aggression?"
- Wrap-up questions: "What's the most important finding from this study?" "Which was the crucial event in determining our success?" "What failures are the most important ones for us to study?" "What have I learned from studying this topic?"

CHAPTER 3

Circular Response

Developed by the adult educator Eduard Lindeman (Brookfield, 1988) in the 1930s, this exercise is designed to help groups narrow the range of possible topics and drill down into a deeper exploration of one or two important themes. It puts a premium on careful listening and informed responding. Because of the anxiety this exercise often produces, we advise against using it at the start of a group's time together.

PURPOSES

· To help a group whose members have multiple agendas and topics to find one or two they can focus on
· To encourage careful active listening

- To enjoy the respect and affirmation of peers as you witness them strive to build on your contribution
- To democratize group deliberation by involving every member in shaping the course of the conversation

HOW IT WORKS

- The facilitator or a group member poses a question for group consideration.
- Whoever wishes to start does so by speaking for up to a minute, responding to the question. No interruptions are allowed. Once the first speaker has finished, the person to the speaker's left then speaks for up to a minute. However, he or she strives to build on the preceding speaker's comments and uses them as a springboard for his or her own contribution.
- The process continues around the circle. As each new person takes a turn to speak, he or she tries to build on the comments of the person before.
- The comments people offer don't have to be in the form of agreements. It's fine to express dissent from, or confusion regarding, the previous speaker's contribution. One might say, "here's why in my experience I haven't found what you say to be true" or "it's difficult for me to respond because I don't understand the terminology you use" and then explain why the experiences or terminology are unfamiliar.
- The facilitator participates but never as the first speaker.
- Once everyone has spoken, the group moves into open conversation with no ground rules. People can pick up on earlier

contributions or take the discussion in a new direction, provide examples, ask questions, make connections, express disagreements or new perspectives, and offer meta-analyses of overarching themes or major differences.

WHERE AND WHEN IT WORKS WELL

Meetings in which listening is not practiced. Because it obliges people to listen to others' views rather than constantly asserting their own, this is a good new discipline to practice in meetings where people come with entrenched perspectives and firm commitments.

When a group has been together some time. This is not a beginning technique. People need a level of familiarity and trust for it to work well.

When groups need to focus on manageable projects. This often gets people to focus on one or two projects that they wish to accomplish.

WHAT USERS APPRECIATE

The organic nature of the conversation. Once members have spoken they tend to lean in and follow the conversation intensely. They want to see how the next speaker responds to their comments and if their points are threaded into the rest of the discussion.

Being treated respectfully. Participants really appreciate when someone tries to respond to them by first listening carefully to what they're saying.

The emphasis on listening. Being obliged to listen carefully to what's being said is a discipline missing from many meetings and discussions.

How it democratizes group process. Everyone gets an equal chance to speak and to determine the direction of the group's deliberations.

WHAT TO WATCH OUT FOR

The powerful should never be the first to speak. If the group is composed of organizational or community members with different positional authority it's important that the senior person *not* be the one to start.

Not leaving enough silence. People often feel pressure to respond immediately to comments they have just heard. Stress that it's fine, even preferable, to take a long pause before responding. When it gets to their turn to speak in the first round, facilitators should think for a while before talking to model the importance of silent thought.

Interruption. It's very difficult to stop people interrupting in this first round, particularly if they want to say "what a fantastic idea!" or "that's so true." Often people want to provide immediate illustrations from their own experience to support a point someone has made. You have to intervene to stop this and emphasize that the point is to listen carefully and to let people express their view however they wish to. Remind them that in the second round of talk they can ask questions, provide examples, underscore agreements, and so on.

Frustration. Individual members get frustrated when themes they want to talk about are not the ones that emerge in the first round. Emphasize that in the second round of talk people can introduce new points, point out overlooked perspectives, and introduce new lines of analysis.

Anxiety. Participants get anxious about not being able to understand the previous speaker's comments and not knowing how to respond. Stress at the outset that taking time to think about a contribution is fine and that it's perfectly legitimate to say, "I'm having a really hard time thinking of anything to say." The important point is that people strive to explain why they find it difficult to respond (for example, they don't know the terminology used or don't share the experiences being disclosed).

Forgetting comments. In the open conversation it's sometimes it's hard to recall all the issues that piqued your interest during the first round of talk.

QUESTIONS SUITED TO THIS TECHNIQUE

- Questions focused on future directions: "Where do we want to be in five years?" "What would it look like for us to function effectively?" "How can we live out our mission?"
- Questions designed to get to the root of what's preventing organizational functioning: "What most stops me from doing good work?" "Why is this initiative stalling?"
- Questions seeking to illustrate the breadth of responses, interpretations, or understandings of a topic: "Why is this hypothesis correct?" "What does it mean to act professionally

here?" "How do you respond to Smith's contention that...?" "What is hegemony?"

· Questions of application: "What are the practical implications of this innovation?" "When have you seen hegemony in your life?" "How does Brown's theory challenge our understanding of topic A?"

· Questions designed to prioritize: "What's the key point or most important finding of this report?" "Which interpretation do you find most convincing or provocative?"

CHAPTER 4

Newsprint Dialogue

This is a silent way of debriefing small-group conversations that enables every individual to engage equally with every finding from the small groups.

PURPOSES

- To eliminate small-group reports that provide spoken summaries of their responses
- To give all participants an equal opportunity to comment on group findings

- To provide a silent approach that accommodates introverts and ESL speakers
- To allow people time to think through responses they wish to make to small-group reports
- To democratize a conversation so no one group or individual exerts disproportionate influence on a discussion
- To create a visual display of the discussion's highlights that can be photographed and preserved

HOW IT WORKS

- In a large class, workshop, or community meeting small groups discuss a common topic, problem, or question.
- Each small group records all the comments, questions, and solutions posed during the discussion on large newsprint sheets. Groups are told everyone will read all comments carefully so they should be as concrete and descriptive as possible.
- Groups post their newsprint sheets around the walls of the room and hang a blank sheet of newsprint next to their posting.
- Each participant is given a marker and told to wander around all the postings and write down on the blank sheet any questions, reactions, agreements, or challenges the postings prompt.
- Often a silence quickly falls on the room as people individually study the postings and react to them.
- After ten minutes or so small groups are told to reconvene at their original postings and talk about the comments people left there. They discuss if they wish to respond to any of the observations made or questions raised.

- The whole group reconvenes and small groups are offered the chance to say anything they wish about the comments added to their original posting. Sometimes nobody has anything to add, in which case the facilitator points out that every person has interacted in a personal way with every item on the original postings and that a thorough debriefing has occurred.
- Before leaving the class or meeting, people are encouraged to take out their phones or tablets and photograph all the postings so these can be the basis of future discussions and agenda building.

WHERE AND WHEN IT WORKS WELL

This is a very adaptable exercise that we have used in multiple settings.

Staff and professional development workshops. We have conducted this in workshops with nonprofits, corporations, hospitals and HMOs, the military, community groups, in churches, schools, colleges, and universities.

Organizational retreats. This is suited to one- or two-day retreats in off-site settings.

Academic classes. It shakes up the humdrum familiarity of the small-group report format.

Community meetings. This technique is especially helpful when citizens are responding to a crisis, such as what to do about hurricane damage, reduce drive-by shootings, control speeding, or stop the closure of a factory or medical facility.

WHAT USERS APPRECIATE

Silence. Introverts appreciate the silence that typically falls on the room when people get their individual markers and start to tour the room reading the postings.

Time to process. For those who need it, there is time to make sense of information and think through how best to post a question or provide a response.

How it equalizes participation. No group's findings have any more prominence than any other group. No one can "speak" louder than anyone else in *Newsprint Dialogue*. Theoretically, the CEO's written postings carry no more weight than the administrative assistant's; the student's has equal weight with the dean's.

No performance anxiety. Because groups are told early on that there will be no conventional small-group reports, they can take the weight of performance anxiety off their shoulders. No one has to worry about sounding smart or choosing a reporter because report-backs to the whole group have been eliminated.

Movement. It gets people out of their chairs and moving around the room. We love to use this as an after-lunch activity!

It creates a permanent record. When a permanent record of the conversation is desired, the newsprint dialogue can be an excellent substitute for minutes.

"We feel heard." Participants love to see their point responded to in print because it confirms that people are interested in what they have to say.

WHAT TO WATCH OUT FOR

Lack of clarity. Sometimes original comments are so brief their meaning is unclear and readers have no sense of the discussion informing them. Despite the instructions to make comments as concrete, specific, and detailed as possible, groups often post just headings with little elaboration and few examples.

Poor sight lines. If the group is too large some people feel crowded out from the process. They can't see the board or get through the crowd to post.

Hostile postings. People reading a posting may ask questions or give reactions that are interpreted by members of the original group as hostile or disrespectful.

Extrovert frustration. Those who like to talk out loud as their way of interpreting data and creating meaning may find it constraining to be in a mostly silent room.

Split verdicts. Be prepared for a split verdict on *Newsprint Dialogue*. Quieter, introverted types tend to love it. Extraverts are often frustrated by what they see as an overreliance on the written word. They want to talk! Just keep in mind that at least a third of the gathering is likely to find it worthwhile.

QUESTIONS SUITED TO THIS TECHNIQUE

· Questions to capture a group's reaction to a report, class reading, or case study

· Questions that ask the members of a group to reflect on a common experience: "What's the best way to respond to resistance?" "When is pushback justified?"

· Questions that focus on good practice: "What are examples of authentic leadership?" "When have we come closest to working democratically?"

CHAPTER 5

Today's Meet

Today's Meet (https://todaysmeet.com/) is an electronic way of getting immediate and anonymous input from group members that can be used to structure discussion, check for understanding, and generate new questions. It can be used with any group size. We have found it works well in meetings or classes of fifteen or twenty people right up to town hall meetings, conference keynotes, workshops, or classes of several hundred.

PURPOSES

· To provide an anonymous opportunity for participants to ask questions, provide reactions, raise issues, offer criticisms, and suggest future directions

- To democratize participation so everyone has an equal opportunity to contribute
- To allow people time to formulate and ask questions or express opinions even if the discussion has moved on
- To create an alternative to small-group reports

HOW IT WORKS

To provide a continuous back channel for participants to raise concerns and pose questions

As facilitator you pull up the *Today's Meet* website (https://todaysmeet.com/) on a screen everyone can see.

- You show them how you create a unique page for the session, giving it a specific name. So, for a session on antiracism your page might be titled, *todaysmeet.com/antiracism.*
- Then you enter your fictional identity for the day. You can use your own name if you wish.
- Participants then access the *Todays' Meet* home page on their phones, tablets, or laptops and create a fictional identity so they can enter comments anonymously.
- You encourage people to use *Today's Meet* to ask questions, give reactions, provide critiques, raise issues, and suggest new directions for the discussion whenever these occur to them. You explain that you will pull up the feed on a screen every fifteen minutes so everyone can see what's been posted. Of course, anyone who is logged in can also view the feed on his or her device.

- At fifteen-minute intervals you address the comments people have posted. You respond to questions, note suggested new directions, deal with criticisms, and ask the group if they would like to respond to anything on the screen.

To hear small group reports

Another use for this tool is to ask small groups to use *Today's Meet* to summarize the main points they discussed or the key questions they raised. Everyone can then review the postings on the screen in lieu of a series of spoken reports.

To get immediate responses to questions you pose

Finally, a third option is to pose a question to a large group. Then, instead of hearing people speak their responses (which privileges the confident extroverts), everyone posts their responses to the question on the *Today's Meet* page you've created. If you ask for a minute or two of silence while people are doing this you will get far greater participation than if you'd gone straight to speech.

WHERE AND WHEN IT WORKS WELL

With very large groups. We originally used this as a way to make keynote speeches with hundreds in the audience much more interactive.

When issues are contentious or controversial. The anonymity this technique provides means that people can offer opinions and responses using a fictional identity. This reduces the fear of being jumped on for saying the wrong thing.

If there is organizational mistrust. *Today's Meet* is welcomed by people who have been burned in the past for saying the wrong thing or not toeing the line because it enables the safe expression of dissent or contradictory views.

To democratize participation. As with *Chalk Talk* (technique 2) no one can dominate the *Today's Meet* feed by raising his or her voice or drowning others out. Consequently you get much more participation than when you invite out-loud comments, reactions, or questions.

WHAT USERS APPRECIATE

The chance to contribute at their own pace. People have the opportunity to ask questions or make points whenever these occur to them, even if the face-to-face session is focusing on something else. It also enables people to formulate and express a thought exactly the way they wish to.

The opportunity to influence the discussion. Even if you rarely speak up in verbal discussions, this tool gives you the chance to shape how the discussion evolves.

Its anonymity. It enables people to make criticisms, ask hard questions, and introduce contentious ideas without fear of reprisal.

The elimination of performance anxiety. In contrast to face-to-face discussions, the pressure to sound smart and highly informed is lessened.

WHAT TO WATCH OUT FOR

Digital divide. Despite the seeming ubiquity of smartphones, tablets, and laptops, there will be some who don't own these devices.

The 140-character restraint. *Today's Meet* allows posts of only 140 characters, so there's a limit to how deep the online discussion can go. It should be used more as an enhancement to face-to-face conversation.

The seduction of the screen. If you keep the *Today's Meet* feed up on a screen everyone can see, it can divert people's attention from what is being said in the moment. That's why we prefer to keep the screen off during the bulk of the discussion and to bring it up only at fifteen-minute intervals.

QUESTIONS SUITED TO THIS TECHNIQUE

Mostly this technique is used to encourage people to ask questions as they occur to them during a discussion. But we also pose specific questions and ask participants to post their responses. Examples are as follows:

- "What is the most important piece of evidence supporting or refuting climate change?"
- "How should we respond to the task force's main conclusion?"
- "What are the elements of a valid proof?"
- "What's an example of commodification?"
- "How should we respond to criticism A?"
- "What have we missed up to now?"
- "What's the key issue we need to focus on?"
- "Are we on track? If not, what should we do?"

CHAPTER 6

Giving Appreciation

The Appreciative Pause–Sticky Note Plaudit

One of the most neglected behaviors in discussion is showing appreciation for contributions that have enhanced our understanding or led to new lines of questioning or thinking. We try to emphasize this in two ways. The *Appreciative Pause* usually happens during a discussion and the *Sticky Note Plaudit* at its conclusion.

PURPOSES

· To build time for expressing appreciation for specific contributions throughout a discussion
· To give people the experience of receiving respectful acknowledgment
· To teach what people find most helpful, informative, or inspiring
· To create greater goodwill and cohesion in a group
· To encourage quieter members to feel they are valued

HOW IT WORKS—*APPRECIATIVE PAUSE*

· At least once in every discussion you call for a pause of a minute or so. During this time the only comments allowed from participants are those that acknowledge how something that someone else said in the discussion (*not* the instructor) has contributed to their learning.
· Appreciations are often given for these types of things:
    · A question that was asked that suggested a whole new line of thinking
    · A comment that clarified something that up to then was confusing
    · A new idea that is intriguing and had not been considered before
    · A comment clarifying the connection between two other ideas or contributions
    · An example that helped increase understanding of a difficult concept

HOW IT WORKS—*STICKY NOTE PLAUDIT*

To provide an audit of what people appreciated

- At the end of a workshop, meeting, or discussion participants write brief notes of appreciation on small sticky notes for actions taken or contributions made by others in the group.
- These are placed on a board or wall where everyone can see them.
- When all the notes are posted group members go to the wall or board to read them.
- Alternatively, you as facilitator can read out the sticky note plaudits to the whole workshop.

To debrief small-group summaries

- An alternative option is to ask people to use sticky notes when small groups display the results of their discussions on newsprint around the room. Participants place sticky notes next to themes or findings they want to discuss further.
- After a few minutes sticky notes become clustered in patterns that provide an immediate visual record of which comments generated the most reaction.
- The whole group then moves into a discussion of these clusters.

WHERE AND WHEN IT WORKS WELL

When women are prominent in the group. We say this with some trepidation, but in our experience women are more inclined than men to show appreciation for others. In highly gendered environments, such as hospitals and elementary schools, structured appreciation works well.

In organizations, teams, communities, and groups where morale is low. Because one of the key inhibitors to working well is feeling unappreciated, this activity can be a crucial starting point for community and team building.

WHAT USERS APPRECIATE

Feeling recognized and affirmed. When another member notices your contribution, you feel respected and acknowledged.

Learning about what's helpful to others. Group members who simultaneously occupy leadership roles outside the group understand better how to support the work of colleagues and supervisees.

Its concreteness. Many appreciations are detailed descriptions of particular actions. Receivers find these useful and often resolve to do them more regularly.

The cohesion it builds. There is often a noticeable change in group tone or tenor after an *Appreciative Pause* or *Sticky Note Plaudit*.

WHAT TO WATCH OUT FOR

Lack of practice. People don't have much practice doing this so, as with many of these exercises, the facilitator should model how to show appreciation. This is especially relevant when a team is facilitating the event and members can express appreciation for each other's contributions.

Lack of specificity. Appreciation works best when it's specific. Comments such as "I like what you said" don't add much to the conversation compared to a specific comment that shows how a particular observation surprised, informed, or inspired.

QUESTIONS THAT FIT THIS PROTOCOL

This exercise doesn't focus on posing questions other than "What do you appreciate that others have contributed to this discussion?"

CHAPTER 7

Rotating Stations

This is a way of debriefing small-group work in which participants stay together in their groups.

PURPOSES

· To ensure that each participant's work is studied intensely by everyone in the class, workshop, or meeting
· To encourage introverts and ESL speakers to participate in exchanging ideas
· To create a permanent record of what was discussed
· To challenge groups to consider multiple perspectives
· To help participants build on earlier responses, thus creating a more organically developing conversation

- To increase the variety, richness, and fun of small-group interactions

HOW IT WORKS

- A question is posed and small groups discuss their responses. We have allotted anywhere from ten to forty-five minutes for this part of the exercise.
- Each group writes a summary of its discussion on provided newsprint paper. The members are encouraged to be as descriptive and specific as possible and also to write legibly.
- Each group then posts its summary on the wall and places one or two blank sheets of newsprint next to it.
- Groups then move into sharing their findings. This begins with each group standing next to its own posting.
- The facilitator asks groups to move clockwise to the next posting on the wall or station. When the group is at this first station the members talk about what's posted there and then write their reactions, comments, questions, agreements, and disagreements directly onto the blank sheet of paper provided.
- After three to five minutes (this can be extended depending on the complexity of the question and original postings) each small group rotates clockwise to the next station. Now, as well as reading the original posting, the group can also read the responses made by another group to that posting.
- At this second station the group discusses the original posting and records its reactions to it, but they also read what the last group wrote and raise questions or add comments about it.

- The process continues around the room with groups developing new threads as they respond to earlier group comments.
- Eventually each group ends up back where it began, at its own station. The members read the reactions of all the other groups to their original posting and spend five minutes talking about these. Is there anything they want to respond to? Are there comments posted that they don't understand? What do they find most interesting about how people have responded to their posting?
- The exercise ends with a large-group debrief in which any participants can talk about the process or comments left by other groups. They can also respond to questions that have been raised about their postings.

WHERE AND WHEN THIS WORKS WELL

In community-based settings. This is an excellent way to hear from virtually everyone in, say, a community planning meeting, and then to get all to comment on each other's ideas. This broadens the range of input and gives everyone a chance to consider what is coming up in small groups.

Academic settings. Students especially enjoy moving around the classroom to see what comments each previous group has left behind. This stimulates lively conversations that reflect a wide range of opinions.

Organizational settings. As in community-based settings, this enables you to hear from a lot of coworkers in a relatively safe and nonthreatening way.

Multiple perspectives in diverse settings. Because groups arrive at each new posting ready to consider what new ideas are written there, they're less likely to miss diverse or dissenting viewpoints.

WHAT USERS APPRECIATE

It democratizes participation. No small-group report gets more airtime in this exercise. People enjoy the intimacy of the small group throughout. All participants have an equal chance to comment on all other group contributions.

It gets people moving. We typically do this for afternoon classes and workshops when people get sleepy and distracted. This is an especially good technique, therefore, to liven up proceedings that have fallen into a rut or in which interaction has been limited.

It provides a permanent record. In meetings, when a permanent record of the conversation is desired, the rotating stations dialogue can be an excellent substitute for minutes.

It encourages organically developing conversation. People have the chance to build on comments made by earlier groups and respond to questions posed.

WHAT TO WATCH OUT FOR

Time to consider the original question. This should be adjusted depending on the question's complexity. A simple question about which people are well informed can be discussed in fifteen minutes. A complex and open-ended one may need up to an hour.

Timing for visiting each station. As groups rotate between postings, monitor their progress and be flexible in determining how long you allow. We typically budget three to five minutes for each rotation.

Legibility and specificity. The first time people try this they often use general phrases and don't give enough detail in the original posting. This improves the next time around.

Getting lost in details. It's easy to get too focused on a particular finding or response. Remind people they should be looking for patterns of agreement, recurring questions, important contradictions, and new issues raised.

The debriefing flops. Sometimes the energy of small-group discussions is followed by awkward silence when the whole group is given the chance to debrief. If so, simply remind participants that a vigorous conversation has already happened. Each group has focused on, discussed, and responded to every other group's work.

QUESTIONS THAT FIT THIS PROTOCOL

· Questions that are open and multidimensional in which you want to discover the different ways people think about an issue or pursue their practice: "What does it mean to act inclusively?" "How can we work more democratically?" "Where does our group, team, or community go from here?"

· Questions asking people to dive into a difficult issue: "What is stopping us from being a learning organization?" "What will help us do our best work?"

· Questions that invite groups to enumerate central qualities of something: "What are the elements of an effective theory?" "What are the key ingredients of student success?"

CHAPTER 8

Snowballing

Snowballing comes from the metaphor of a snowball rolling down a hill. At the top it's a small ball but as it descends it gathers pace to become bigger until arriving at the bottom as a large globe. A snowballing discussion begins with individual reflection followed by sharing in ever-larger groups until everyone is involved. Earlier themes become expanded, deepened, and reconfigured as the group size increases.

PURPOSES

· To make sure everyone gets a chance to participate
· To provide a range of modalities in one experience—individual reflection, paired exchange, small-group discussion, and whole-class or workshop analysis

- To ensure that discussion progresses organically, with early themes and questions being threaded through larger and larger conversations

HOW IT WORKS

- As facilitator, chair, or leader you pose a question for the group to consider or the group poses an issue the members wish to discuss.
- People begin with a minute or two of silent reflection to organize their initial thoughts.
- The facilitator then asks people to share their initial thoughts with one other person.
- After a few minutes, pairs are asked to find another pair and to share emerging responses to the question. You stress that people should look for differences, new questions being raised, and issues that are beginning to emerge.
- After another few minutes, quartets are asked to join up to form octets. Again, each quartet shares differences, issues, and new questions being expressed.
- The process continues as increasingly larger groups are formed.
- The exercise ends when the sharing has reached the point when everyone is involved. The largest group size we have tried this with is about sixty-five people.

WHERE AND WHEN IT WORKS WELL

If you want to democratize group process. At some point in *Snowballing* everyone has contributed something to the ongoing conversation.

If you want a conversation to build organically. Properly conducted, *Snowballing* enables themes to build gradually as new groups use previous group contributions as their starting point.

WHAT USERS APPRECIATE

The initial intimacy. We often hear that the sharing in pairs was the best part of this exercise.

The organic development of themes. As groups get larger the introverts and ESL speakers get quieter. However, it's gratifying for them to see their questions and issues being taken up by the larger group.

The chance to work with everyone else in the room. The logic of *Snowballing* is that each participant ultimately ends up in a group discussion with every other person.

The diversity of perspectives that are revealed. When groups share disagreements, issues, and questions with each other, the range of perspectives explored often surprises people.

The physical movement. Each time groups convene with each other, people have to rearrange chairs and tables, cross the room, and move their bodies. This is a good interruption to the fatigue that can result from people sitting too long.

WHAT TO WATCH OUT FOR

Declining participation. As groups increase in size the participation rate drops precipitously. Usually there is reasonable participation up to the octets, but beyond that the usual confident extroverts tend to dominate. However, the themes that are talked about in larger groups often originate in an introvert's comments shared in a pair or quartet.

Uneven numbers. The exercise works optimally in a group of thirty-two or sixty-four people. Because that perfect size is rare, you have to make adjustments as the exercise progresses.

Too much summarizing. When groups get together with new groups they often provide a précis of what they've been talking about. Remind groups that when they convene with others they should highlight differences and disagreements they've observed, new questions posed, and any issues emerging from their conversations.

QUESTIONS SUITED TO THIS TECHNIQUE

As with any good question there should be a legitimate range of reactions and interpretations that can be given in response. The question also needs to be one that everyone can weigh in on, either because they know the material or have experience with the topic.

- "What's the most important finding of this research?"
- "Which part of our mission statement do we most need to work on implementing?"
- "Of the hypotheses we've examined, which makes the most sense to test?"
- "What do we stand for as a community?"
- "How do we judge which of the theories we've examined is most useful?"

CHAPTER 9

Conversational Moves

Conversational Moves provides an opportunity for people to practice genuinely reciprocal discussion based on careful listening and responding by providing very specific examples of different ways to enact such a discussion. This exercise works well with technique 49, *Conversational Roles,* because the moves are specific enactments of the roles we suggest people play.

PURPOSES

· To broaden awareness of what counts as good participation in discussion

- To give participants practice in performing specific discussion actions
- To make discussion a collaborative endeavor in which acknowledging and strengthening connections among group members are emphasized
- To alert participants to underused discussion actions such as expressing gratitude, consciously using body language, and asking for silence

HOW IT WORKS

- The facilitator prepares a number of different conversational moves and puts these on different slips of paper. Each move is a specific behavior or action someone might enact during a discussion. Typical moves include the following:
    - Ask a question or make a comment that shows you are interested in what another person says.
    - Ask a question or make a comment that encourages another person to elaborate on a previous observation.
    - Make a comment that underscores the link between two people's contributions.
    - Use body language to show interest in what different speakers are saying.
    - Comment specifically on how another person's ideas were helpful or useful.
    - Contribute something that explicitly builds on or springs from what someone else has said.
    - Make a comment that paraphrases and credits what another person has said.

- Make a summary observation that takes into account several people's contributions and touches on a recurring theme in the discussion.
- When you think it's appropriate, ask the group for a moment's silence to slow the pace of conversation and give you and others time to think.
- Use specific examples to express appreciation for the value you have gained from the conversation.
- Disagree with someone respectfully and constructively.
- Create a space for someone who has not yet spoken to make a contribution.

- Before the discussion begins, the moves are placed face down or folded over in the middle of the table or room. Group members randomly choose a notecard containing their move, which is an instruction to take a specific action at least once during the course of the discussion. They are told not to disclose their move to the group.
- Participants then hold a discussion about the day's question or topic. They can participate in any way they wish but are told to make their move whenever the opportunity arises. This should not be forced, and people are told that they may never have the chance to make their move.
- When the discussion is over, members are invited to share their moves with the group and to talk about how challenging it was to behave in the way specified.

WHERE AND WHEN IT WORKS WELL

It expands the repertoire of discussion behaviors. This works well to change discussion dynamics. Asking for a pause in the conversation, showing appreciation for how a contribution has helped you understand something better, or explicitly building on another person's comments all make discussions more reciprocal. **When you are trying to introduce discussion.** The specific moves help guide new discussants to enact helpful discussion behaviors.

WHAT USERS APPRECIATE

It's creative energy. We've used this with a New York City theatre group that escorts low-income youth to Broadway plays and then holds post-play discussions with them. Facilitators reported this to be unusually energizing.

Specificity. People like the concreteness of the different moves described.

Reassuring structure. Far from being restrictive, participants typically appreciate the direction this technique provides about what is expected of them in discussion-based classrooms.

WHAT TO WATCH OUT FOR

Performance anxiety. Some participants are so anxious about the move they are expected to make that they can't really focus on what is transpiring in the discussion as a whole. Emphasize that making the move is not the point of the discussion. You do this only if an opportunity arises.

Gimmicky. Some see this as gimmicky, even as others enjoy its specificity, so don't devote too much time to it. Give people a brief taste of it by keeping the actual discussion to no more than fifteen minutes.

Skipping the end sharing. It's important for everyone to share what move they were instructed to make. Hearing about these and the challenge of enacting them reinforces the variety of ways we can add to a discussion.

QUESTIONS THAT FIT THIS PROTOCOL

This approach can be used with any type of question.

CHAPTER 10

Critical Incident Questionnaire (CIQ)

The *Critical Incident Questionnaire (CIQ)* is a one-page, five-item instrument that provides anonymous feedback on how discussions are progressing.

PURPOSES

· To provide regular, valid information on how people experience discussions

- To help facilitators judge the accuracy of their assumptions about what best helps people learn
- To detect problems early before they get out of hand
- To help participants appreciate the range of learning preferences in a group
- To model critical thinking by instructors and leaders
- To keep resistance in accurate perspective

HOW IT WORKS

- At the end of a class, meeting, workshop, or staff training the facilitator hands out a form containing the following five questions:
  - "At what moment were you most engaged as a learner?"
  - "At what moment were you most distanced as a learner?"
  - "What action was taken that was most helpful to your learning?"
  - "What action was taken that was most puzzling to you?"
  - "What surprised you most about the session today?"
- Participants are told *not* to put their names on the form and that the responses will be summarized when the class, meeting, or workshop reconvenes.
- The forms take three to five minutes to fill out and a volunteer collects and hands them to the facilitator.
- Before the group reconvenes the facilitator reads the forms and summarizes the main responses. Any item or event mentioned by at least 10 percent of the participants makes it onto the summary.
- When the group reconvenes, or sooner if electronically possible, the facilitator gives a report on the CIQ responses, noting

the main themes that emerged, any changes contemplated in response to CIQ feedback, and which assumptions about how facilitators help learning were affirmed or challenged.

· The group and facilitator discusses the responses and any changes proposed.

WHERE AND WHEN IT WORKS WELL

This is remarkably adaptable, and we've used it in multiple organizational, community, and academic settings.

Anytime a group meets more than once. The CIQ is used only if a group meets more than once because reporting back people's responses and discussing how these influence what happens next is its central dynamic. It's not really suited to a short, one-off event such as a two-hour training or a single community forum.

In one-day events. This can be adapted to one-day seminars or workshops in which the CIQ can be filled out just before lunch. The facilitator studies the responses over lunch and starts the afternoon with a report on the morning's CIQs.

WHAT USERS APPRECIATE

It heads off resistance before it gets out of control. The CIQ alerts leaders, teachers, and chairs to any problems that exist while they are still nascent. It's an early-warning device for addressing emerging difficulties.

It provides solid, reliable information that helps you make informed decisions. Instead of relying on instincts and observations, your decisions are based on evidence coming from the participants themselves.

61

It democratizes participation. Everyone has the same opportunity on the CIQ to influence the course of events.

It lets people know the diversity of realities in the room. The reporting of results enables participants to see that the same event was experienced multiple ways and that the same content was interpreted very differently. This stops people universalizing their own experience and assuming everyone thinks like they do.

It helps teachers and leaders justify their use of multiple approaches. Because a diversity of experience and interpretation is revealed, the CIQ strengthens the argument that no single approach or activity should predominate.

It models critical thinking. As the results are being reported the teacher or leader can share how the results confirm or challenge the assumptions he or she holds about how best to help learning or run meetings. Facilitators can also describe the new perspectives that the CIQ results suggest to them.

It keeps resistance in perspective. Resistance manifested by a few extroverts can easily be interpreted as the only reaction people are having to a class, meeting, or workshop. The CIQ helps you understand that this may be much less widespread than you assume and underscores how quieter students are benefitting.

WHAT TO WATCH OUT FOR

Focusing only on negative comments. In the effort to feel they are reaching everyone, facilitators can spend too long dealing with a small percentage of criticisms.

Taking too long to give your report. Sometimes people are anxious to get going with the agenda, especially if the CIQ responses largely document that most people are happy with how things are going.

Always doing what the majority wants. Often a majority of group members will dislike an activity that a minority finds helpful. For example, extroverts will dislike the enforced silence of *Chalk Talk*. But if a minority is finding something helpful it is important to stand firm and say that a variety of approaches will be retained in the interests of reaching every participant.

Negotiation not capitulation. Sometimes you will get only negative responses, for example, when you refuse to tell people the correct answer and ask them to think things out for themselves. At other times people will resist your agenda strongly, as when all White groups resist dealing with racial micro-aggressions. At such times you need to acknowledge participant opposition but also explain why you will not budge from your agenda.

People using the CIQ to get other participants. If people complain about a specific member who is identified, we do not report that in the way it's stated. Instead we reframe the personal criticism as a general dynamic that needs to be addressed. So, instead of reporting that "three people described Joe as dominating" we will report that "three identified a need to ensure that everyone has a chance to talk."

QUESTIONS THAT FIT THIS PROTOCOL

This is a formative evaluation tool, and the questions are those noted on the form.

CHAPTER 11

Strategic Questioning

Listening, questioning, and responding are the foundation of good discussion. Learning to question well is a hard skill to learn, requiring an awareness of how to ask different kinds of questions. *Strategic Questioning* invites participants to partake in an exercise designed to give them practice in varying their questioning approaches.

PURPOSES

- To encourage more questioning by all discussion participants
- To practice a repertoire of different question approaches that promotes deeper consideration of a topic

- To teach how to ask questions that are regarded as exploratory, not accusatory
- To underscore the role thoughtful questioning plays in advancing discussion

HOW IT WORKS

- Facilitators introduce a range of question types designed to deepen discussion—together these types of questions form the mnemonic CLOSE-UP:

  Clarity. "What do you mean by that? Can you put that another way?"

  Linking. "How is that similar to what we read earlier? How does your view compare to Amalfi's?"

  Open-ended. "What's happening here? What interests you about this issue?"

  Synthesis. "What stands out from what we discussed? What big question still lingers?"

  Evidence. "How did you come to know this? What experience is your analysis based on?"

  Understanding. "Why do you think this is happening? How do you explain this situation?"

  Priority. "What matters to you most about this? What's the most important value or principle we should consider here?"

- People form into triads, and each person takes a turn as the sharer, questioner, and observer.
- Someone provides a topic for consideration: "What constitutes good practice?" "When are we at our best as a community or

organization?" "What's the most important finding of this research?" "What does the text mean to you?" "How can we use this report to improve what we're doing?"

· In each triad the sharer gives his or her initial response to the question and the questioner poses different types of questions from CLOSE-UP to draw out the sharer.

· The observer takes note of what transpires, keeping track of the different kinds of questions asked. After five minutes the triad pauses and the observer notes the variety of questions posed.

· The exercise is then repeated but with the roles switched. After another five minutes the exercise is done a final time, again with the roles being switched. This way everyone is a sharer, a questioner, and an observer.

· The whole group reconvenes to give the members' reactions to the exercise and to assess their ability to ask different kinds of questions.

WHERE AND WHEN IT WORKS WELL

When gaining skill as a questioner is important. Teachers, trainers, professional development coordinators, and community activists all need to know how to vary questions to keep discussion going.

With groups lacking questioning experience. Groups that have been discouraged from voicing members' ideas in a public setting can interrogate public officials more effectively.

With college and university teachers. This shows students how good questions can enliven any academic setting.

WHAT USERS APPRECIATE

Acquiring a repertoire of questions. Having an easily recalled array of question types to draw on helps people ask more and better questions.

Recognizing the power of questioning. Users are often surprised how much good information emerges from a five-minute conversation using a range of questions.

WHAT TO WATCH OUT FOR

Not getting hung up on asking all seven types of questions. There is no need to cover all the question types. If three or four different formats are used that's fine.

The sharer gets on a roll. If the topic is especially engaging to the sharer, she or he may become so animated there is little opportunity to ask questions. Questioners should be urged to take an active role in the conversation, interrupting occasionally to steer the exchange in new directions. But even if one particular exchange doesn't go exactly as planned, doing this three times increases the chance that everyone will have one interaction that is driven by good questions.

Skipping the debriefing. If the conversation is intensely interesting to participants there is a risk of it going on so long that there is no time to debrief in small or large groups. Make sure you allot time for this. The point of the exercise is to raise awareness of, and provide opportunities for, different questioning approaches. It's crucial to keep the focus on how doing so enriches understanding and opens up new possibilities, and the debriefing is essential to this.

QUESTIONS THAT FIT THIS PROTOCOL

· Questions that invite people to reflect on their personal experiences: "How do you know your students or colleagues are learning?" "What's a good day at work look like to you?"

· Questions that prompt participants to respond to a short article, report, or case study: "What's the most important finding of this research?" "What does the text mean to you?" "How can we use this report to improve what we're doing?"

· Questions that ask people to take a stance on some issue and to explain their reasons for that stance: "When are we at our best as a community or organization?" "How can we make this a more inclusive workplace?" "How should we evaluate good performance and learning progress?"

CHAPTER 12

Open-ended Questions

A variant on technique 11, *Strategic Questioning*, this exercise alerts people to a tendency to rely on closed questions and asks them to turn these into generative, open-ended questions.

PURPOSES

- To alert participants to the frequency with which closed questions are posed
- To provide practice in distinguishing between open-ended and closed questions

- To help people learn how to turn closed questions into a more generative format
- To change perceptions that open-ended questions are too loose and unfocused

HOW IT WORKS

- In small groups of four or five members, participants are presented with ten questions on a topic. Some are clearly open-ended, some clearly closed, and some are somewhat ambiguous.
- Members discuss the guidelines they will use to distinguish between open-ended and closed questions.
- Possible guidelines include that open-ended questions have no single, final answer, whereas closed questions usually do; open questions often start with "why" or "how" and closed questions often begin with "what," "who," or "when"; the answers to closed questions can be easily researched, whereas open questions are usually too complicated for this and need extensive research; closed questions usually have objective, factual answers, whereas open questions often invite responses based on personal experience.
- Using these guidelines, groups label each of the prepared questions with either an O (open-ended), a C (closed), or an A (ambiguous).
- Once questions are labeled, groups revise the questions so that the C and A questions are converted to O questions.
- Using all of the questions they have developed, each group chooses the open-ended question that has the greatest potential for fostering lively discussion.

· The exercise ends with groups conducting technique 1, *Circle of Voices,* using the single question chosen.

WHERE AND WHEN IT WORKS WELL

With young people. Because this exercise is loosely based on one stage of the *question formulation technique* developed by K–12 educators Rothstein and Santana (2011), this works well in schools and youth-oriented community settings.

In organizational meetings. Practicing the habit of asking mostly open-ended questions generates new topics and new avenues for discussion.

In team and community assessment. Along with assessment protocols tied to the accomplishment of predefined goals, *Open-Ended Questions* helps capture unintended consequences and overlooked achievements.

In facilitator, leader, and teacher-training workshops. We often use this exercise in workshops on creativity and inclusiveness for facilitators, leaders, and teachers.

WHAT USERS APPRECIATE

Its creativity and openness. Students appreciate open-ended questions for stimulating thinking and opening up discussion, removing pressure to guess the correct answer.

How it promotes feelings of equality. When there is no single right answer, everyone is on roughly the same level in addressing the question.

Practicality. Distinguishing between closed and open questions reinforces the value of open questions and how they can be formulated more readily.

WHAT TO WATCH OUT FOR

Fretting over the question types. Sometimes there is no clear-cut way to settle on question type, especially those appearing to be ambiguous. Remind people not to spend too long on this. The primary purpose is to give people concrete practice reframing questions to make them more open-ended.

Wanting to know if the "right" guidelines have been developed. Talking through the criteria to distinguish open-ended from closed questions can sometimes take up the bulk of the time available. Let groups know when it's time to move into classifying particular questions.

Choosing the best question. At the end of the exercise, when the group is trying to settle on a question to discuss briefly, the members might find themselves caught between three or four questions they like. Again, let groups know that just the act of deliberating over this issue is the point, not whether they actually chose the "right" question.

Pointlessness. Because this is not tied to solving an immediate problem, people often need to be persuaded that it's worth spending time doing this to prepare for future problem-solving discussions.

QUESTIONS THAT FIT THIS PROTOCOL

This exercise is about turning closed and ambiguous questions into open-ended ones so the questions you use will vary according to context and setting. Using this book as an example, closed question examples are "Should this book be used to train discussion facilitators?" "Is it justified to call on people to speak?" Open question examples are "What do good discussions look like?" "What do discussion facilitators need to know to be effective?" Ambiguous question examples are "How can this book be used to train our facilitators?" "How will this book solve our communication problems?"

CHAPTER 13

Nominating Questions

When moving from small- to large-group discussions it's sometimes difficult to decide what should be the focus of the large-group discussion. *Nominating Questions* addresses this concern by inviting participants to vote for which question or questions will be the focus for whole-group exploration.

PURPOSES

- To give participants control over the focus of large-group discussion
- To provide small groups practice in developing engaging questions for large-group discussion

- To avoid the loss of energy that sometimes afflicts reporting back to a group
- To ensure an organic connection between small- and large-group discussions

HOW IT WORKS

- Small groups engage in a discussion of a topic or focus question.
- One person volunteers to keep a list of questions that emerge during the discussion.
- As they conclude their discussions the recorder shares the questions raised so far. Group members voice any additional questions they would like to have considered.
- The group then chooses one or two questions that emerged from its conversation that they would like the large group to discuss.
- Each group puts its questions on the blackboard or on newsprint. This can also be done electronically via *Today's Meet* (https://todaysmeet.com).
- Each participant is then invited to come to the board and put a check or sticky note by the question he or she most wants to discuss.
- The questions that receive the most votes then become the focus of the whole-group conversation.

WHERE AND WHEN IT WORKS WELL

When moving from small- to large-group discussion. This is a good exercise in any class, workshop, or meeting in which you are looking for a relatively simple but meaningful transition from small-group deliberations to large-group discussion.

Building an agenda. This is useful whenever you're trying to build an agenda from the ground floor or grass roots. People like to feel in control of the topics they are discussing.

When democratic fairness is important. This democratizes a process so that no group exerts undue influence.

WHAT USERS APPRECIATE

The chance to exert control. Participants get to influence the direction of the large-group discussion.

The fairness of the process. Everyone can see that the questions generating the most interest become the focus for subsequent discussion.

Knowing that their small-group work matters. People know that what they do in the small group will not disappear into the ether but will be considered in what happens next.

WHAT TO WATCH OUT FOR

Shortchanging the time in the small group to develop questions. If a small group is engaged in an interesting and intense discussion it's often hard to get the members to step back and identify possible questions that have emerged. This is why the question recorder is so important.

Keeping the large-group discussion focused. Once the top questions have been identified it's crucial that the facilitator strives to ensure that the subsequent large-group discussion stays focused on these.

QUESTIONS THAT FIT THIS PROTOCOL

The focus question that triggers the small-group discussions from which nominating questions subsequently emerge must be complex and controversial enough to stimulate a variety of interesting questions for further large-group conversation. Examples of focus questions are as follows:

· "How would our organizations and communities look different if discussion were more highly valued?"
· "How can we democratize our organization or community?"
· "What would it mean to function as a learning organization?"
· "What future strategies can ensure our group's long-term stability?"

CHAPTER 14

If You Could Only Ask One Question

This activity focuses on the first part of the questioning-listening-responding dynamic that is so essential to good discussion. It asks small groups to generate only one question that they think enables them to go deeper into an issue or promotes greater understanding of content.

PURPOSES

- To demonstrate the power of a single question
- To practice asking questions that help a discussion build organically

- To generate questions that open up new avenues for exploration of a topic or issue
- To promote greater understanding of that topic
- To gauge the nature of questions that seem to spur the most discussion

HOW IT WORKS

- We like to introduce this exercise by offering two examples.
    - First a scene from the film *Color of Fear* (1994) is shown in which the facilitator, Lee Mun Wah, asks a white male participant in a racism workshop what is keeping him from believing what others have shared about the harshness of racism. He then follows up with a provocative question: "What would it mean to you if it were really that harsh?"
    - Second, we watch what Bryan Stevenson, the author of *Just Mercy* (2014) said in his 2012 "TED Talk": "I represent people on death row. It's interesting, this question of the death penalty. In many ways we've been taught to think that the real question is, do people deserve to die for the crimes they've committed? And that's a very sensible question. But the other way of thinking about this is not do people deserve to die for the crimes they've committed, but—do we deserve to kill?"
- The whole group then talks about the examples and how a single question can build deeper understanding of a topic or open people up to new perspectives.
- Next the facilitator introduces a new topic by giving a brief presentation on it or showing a provocative film clip.
- Participants then spend time on their own thinking about questions they would ask that would widen or deepen the subsequent discussion of the topic.

- Small groups of five or six participants share these questions with each other and, time permitting, pose one or two to see what kind of discussion these stimulate.
- The whole group reconvenes and small groups share the questions that worked best.

WHERE AND WHEN IT WORKS WELL

Asking a single good question can galvanize a group almost everywhere.

Academic settings. Many instructors emphasize the importance of students asking good questions and use Socratic questioning, so this suits colleges and universities.

Organizations. For corporate and nonprofit organizations the idea of asking one transformative question fits many of their leadership models.

Community groups and social movements Activists such as Myles Horton, Saul Alinsky, and Paulo Freire are known for asking pivotal, ground-breaking questions, so this shows how these questions are well received in community-based organizations.

WHAT USERS APPRECIATE

Practitioners in action. Seeing activists like Lee Mun Wah and Bryan Stevenson pose their transformative questions motivates participants to attempt this.

Small-group practice. Users appreciate the opportunity to practice coming up with their own game-changing questions but to do so in small groups in which there is less pressure to demonstrate their brilliance.

83

The power of questions. Many participants come to see how powerful a single question can be, an experience that often takes them by surprise.

WHAT TO WATCH OUT FOR

Frustration. Asking the right question at the right time is challenging. Urge people to keep at it because the more they bounce ideas off one another, the easier it gets.

Timing. This exercise is much richer if the small groups have time to test out the viability of the questions by starting to answer them in their groups.

Choosing good examples. We use examples from *Color of Fear* and Bryan Stevenson's "TED Talk" but we encourage you to use other examples that fit your context better. The key point is that they should illustrate the power of asking a single question. Video clips are especially effective at holding a group's attention.

QUESTIONS THAT FIT THIS PROTOCOL

The examples we give in the "How It Works" section are arguably derived from two important categories of questions:

· Questions that ask us to practice technique 34, *Methodological Belief*: "What would it mean for our own lives if another person's experience we had resisted believing turned out to be true?"
· Questions that personalize a big issue: "What would I have done if asked to hide a slave in antebellum America or a Jew in Nazi Germany even though it would have been against the law to do so in both cases?"

- Questions that entertain the opposite or reverse of conventional wisdom on a topic: "In place of 'Do death row criminals deserve to die?' the question becomes, 'Do we deserve to kill?'"
- Questions that broaden ourselves and think beyond our own personal experience: an example might be a question Myles Horton often asked "If I want something desirable for myself and believe I deserve it, shouldn't I want that same thing for all others, especially those far less privileged than me?"

CHAPTER 15

On-the-Spot Questions and Topics

Drawing on the work of Christopher Phillips (2001) and others who have popularized Socrates café, groups of ten to twelve generate a question on the spot that will be the focus of an open, critical, and freewheeling forty-five-minute conversation.

PURPOSES

- To put the decision about the discussion topic under group member control

- To practice holding a discussion on a question of mutual interest without preparation or the need for additional materials
- To learn how to clarify areas of agreement and disagreement in discussions of questions generated on the spot by a group
- To structure discussions so that everyone actively participates

HOW IT WORKS

- Each member of the group brings one question for possible discussion.
- People offer their questions and the facilitator writes these on newsprint.
- Questions tend to be very broad, open-ended questions that just about everyone can relate to, such as, "Why question?" "What is wisdom?" "What is home?" "What gives life meaning?" "How do you know when you know yourself?"
- By consensus or simple voting, the group chooses one question to be discussed.
- The facilitator can help reword or reframe this to make it clear and help people stay focused. For instance, Phillips (2001) shows how a question blurted out at the beginning of one dialogue—"How can a sensitive, intelligent person get stuck in a lousy job"—gets reframed as "What does it mean to be stuck and what, if anything, can done about it?"
- The discussion commences and facilitator and participants use key questions to keep the discussion going:
  - "What do you mean by that?"
  - "What's your definition?"

- "How do you know?"
- "How did you come to believe that?"
- "What do you think?"
- "What would you like to add to what we have already heard?"
- "How certain are you about this?"
- "As we come to the end of this discussion, what stands out for you and why?"
- Final questions might be as follows:
  - "What do you understand better as a result of this discussion?"
  - "What are you even more confused about as a result of this discussion?"
  - "What new questions came up for you?"
  - "What would be a good question to follow up the conversation we're finishing?"

WHERE AND WHEN IT WORKS WELL

When foundational thinking is required. These dialogues can be useful in organizational and community settings in which participants need to be reminded of the mission or core principles guiding their work.

With groups who don't know each other. Socrates cafés work best in public settings when people are strangers

When there are few time constraints. Everyone should be comfortable with not solving a problem or definitively answering a question. We do not recommend this approach in tense organizational situations in which a crisis needs addressing or for a high-stakes program review.

For team building. Generating on-the-spot, open-ended questions and topics helps build relationships.

To widen perspectives. This activity usually opens up new viewpoints on a problem.

WHAT USERS APPRECIATE

Topic control. Participants control what gets discussed, giving them a sense of empowerment.

Question refinement. Users often note that framing the question well beforehand makes for a better subsequent conversation.

The joy of freewheeling dialogue. The chance to participate in a dialogue with relative strangers about a mutually chosen topic is an exhilarating and enjoyable experience.

WHAT TO WATCH OUT FOR

Going off topic. A series of tangential comments can lead the group astray, so facilitator and alert participants must keep reminding everyone of the original question.

Uneven participation. These dialogues work best when lots of people participate. Use technique 48 (the three-person rule) when necessary and watch for body language and eye contact from those trying to join in.

Model questioning. As facilitator, almost all your participation should involve asking questions. This helps to keep the conversation moving, draws out more participants, and sets an example for others who may follow your lead.

QUESTIONS THAT FIT THIS PROTOCOL

The kinds of questions that work best were noted in the "How It Works" section:

- "Why question?"
- "What is wisdom?"
- "What is home?"
- "What gives life meaning?"
- "How do you know when you know yourself?"

However, there are many similar questions that could be adopted.

CHAPTER 16

What Do *You* Think?

In many discussions you as the facilitator are trying to stay above the fray so participants can wrestle with a complex issue in which no clearly right answer exists. In such situations people will eventually confront you directly and ask what you think. Yet you may well be reluctant to answer for fear of inducing colleagues, students, and community members to parrot your view as the right one. This technique enables you to give your opinion while still asking people to engage with multiple viewpoints.

PURPOSES

- To show that you respect participant eagerness to know what you think
- To give your opinion in a way that doesn't unduly bias subsequent conversation
- To engage people in thinking through how they judge the reasoning behind another's comments

HOW IT WORKS

- When a group insists that you give your opinion, you tell them you will provide two or three possible answers, one of which represents your actual opinion. You also say you are going to ask people to choose which answer they feel actually represents your true belief.
- You then give two or three plausible responses that represent different views on the issue. Standing at different stations in the room as you express each opinion helps.
- After hearing your responses participants vote on which of them represents your actual opinion. People then go and stand at the station representing their vote.
- At their stations you ask people to talk for two or three minutes about the reasons for their answer choice. Some choose a response because they've heard you express something similar before, some because it makes the most sense, or some because it seems to tally with expert opinion or a consensus in the field.
- The different groups then present the reasons why they chose the response they did.

· You reveal which of the responses represents your actual position and talk about the group reasons for choosing views you do not hold.

WHERE AND WHEN IT WORKS WELL

When teaching critical thinking. This can be instructive in assessing the assumptions and overall reasoning that underlie different viewpoints.

When trying to get people to make independent judgments. This exercise gives participants practice in not adopting opinions just because they are held by authority figures.

WHAT USERS APPRECIATE

Putting the facilitator on the spot. Participants often enjoy seeing the leader struggle to provide equally plausible yet opposing positions.

Not keeping the facilitator's views a secret. Many users appreciate it when leaders agree to answer their question, albeit in a convoluted and roundabout way!

Making criteria visible. It's helpful to explore the criteria all of us use to judge whether a discussant's comments honestly and plausibly reflect her or his views.

WHAT TO WATCH OUT FOR

Doing this with unimportant issues. This exercise should be used only when you need people to grapple with major issues and learn how to respond. When overdone with smaller issues, it becomes tiring and predictable.

Not having convincingly plausible alternative responses. When the question "what do you think?" is sprung on you out of the blue it's often difficult to come up with different plausible answers on the spot. If that's the case, avoid this exercise.

Clearly favoring one of your responses. No matter how much you strive to give each answer with similar conviction and animation, there are sometimes subtle indications (tone of voice, degree of eye contact) that reveal your preferences.

QUESTIONS SUITED TO THIS TECHNIQUE

This is not really a question-generating technique but more a way of asking learners to assess the relative plausibility of different responses you have provided.

CHAPTER 17

Clearness Committee

This is a close listening and questioning exercise, drawing on the work of Parker Palmer (2007) and the traditions of Quaker practice. At its root is the belief that we can discover answers to difficult problems with appropriate support from peers, friends, and colleagues.

PURPOSES

- To help people find their own solutions to their own problems
- To learn to listen and question solely to support the growth of others

- To practice using open-ended, nonjudgmental, and nonleading questioning

HOW IT WORKS

- Small groups are formed of about six to seven participants each.
- One person agrees to be the "holder of the problem" who describes a troubling issue at work for five to eight minutes.
- Another agrees to be the observer who notes the interactions and shares impressions when the process is completed.
- The exercise begins with group members querying the holder of the problem using honest, open, nonjudgmental, and non-leading questions. Every question should be one in which the questioner has no idea what the answer is. Questioners are told to avoid analyzing the problem or giving advice.
- Questioners are told to take time to think, become comfortable with silence, and pose questions that seem to emerge organically from the situation.
- Occasionally, the facilitator may step in to disallow questions that are not sufficiently open or nonjudgmental.
- The holder can choose to ignore those questions that are uncomfortable or unanswerable and to make comments and offer reflections throughout.
- The questioning usually continues for up to thirty minutes.
- When the exercise is over, the whole group explores these issues:
  - What made it hard to ask open, honest, natural questions?
  - How successful do questioners think they were in supporting the storyteller?
  - Did the storyteller gain new clarity on the issue?
  - What were the impressions of the observer?

WHERE AND WHEN IT WORKS WELL

In settings where people already know each other fairly well. When questioners know the holder of the problem and are aware of organizational or community history, the questions posed can often be richer than among strangers

When enough time is allowed to do the process justice. This shouldn't be rushed. It needs plenty of silence, and if there isn't the time to allow good questions to emerge naturally then it probably should be avoided.

In problem-solving community and organizational workshops. Holders of the problem usually describe something that drains their energy or prevents a team from achieving its goal, so this is well suited to meetings convened to troubleshoot problems.

In retreats. The relaxed nature of retreats and the greater time these involve make the *Clearness Committee* well suited to this setting.

In general, this process is attractive to people because it gives them a chance to work together as a community and to be helpful by focusing very intensely on one person's challenging situation. They seem to enjoy learning about those situations and are stimulated by the challenge of using questions to help the storyteller reframe his or her problem.

WHAT USERS APPRECIATE

Being heard. This exercise means holders of the problem experience an intense focus on their story and their responses. It feels wonderful to have people striving to understand your problem and help you find responses to it.

The chance to know colleagues better. As the exercise progresses the holder invariably discloses many aspects of her experiences that are new to the questioners. We often hear questioners say how many new things they discovered about a long-time colleague.

Working as a team. People like working as a focused team to help a colleague with a challenging situation.

Practice formulating questions. Questioners can formulate questions without being rushed or needing to fill silences.

Problem solving. Problem holders leave thinking more clearly about the problem.

WHAT TO WATCH OUT FOR

Frustration at not being able to give advice. Questioners get frustrated at not being able to give advice to solve their colleague's problem. Keep stressing the exercise is designed to help people work these things out for themselves.

Lack of a clear solution. Most complex problems don't have clear or obvious solutions. If they did they wouldn't be complex! You need to let people know going in that this exercise rarely yields one simple resolution.

Difficulty at asking questions with no clue about the answers. People find it hard to formulate questions without some hunch about the answer.

Don't skip the modeling. Try to model this process for participants with a colleague, taking alternate roles and never telling each other in advance what the problem is.

Feeling awkward about silence. Questioners need time to formulate good questions and holders need time to think about their responses and reflect on what these mean. This exercise has many silent, thoughtful pauses. If you model this process with a colleague, show you're comfortable with silence.

Our adaptation is a greatly abbreviated version of the *Clearness Committee*. Our version of this technique is adapted. Actual *Clearness Committees* sometimes go on for three or four hours! Also, committee members typically read a lengthy briefing paper beforehand prepared by the problem holder instead of hearing a brief problem description.

QUESTIONS THAT FIT THIS PROTOCOL

The general question that is traditionally used in this exercise goes something like this: "What challenging problem in your personal or professional life leaves you uncertain about choices or next steps to resolve the situation?"

CHAPTER 18

Team Modeling

One of our core beliefs as educators and leaders is that we have a responsibility to model for people the kinds of behaviors and actions we are looking for. This is particularly important when people are trying to learn new ways of thinking and acting, as would be the case with technique 21, *Participation Rubric*. If we ask people to break old conversational patterns then we need to provide examples of what we're looking for. This is why we much prefer to run workshops, teach classes, and convene meetings as a team. Working this way, we can strive to model the elements of good discussion.

PURPOSES

·   To model the behaviors in the *Participation Rubric* (technique 21)
·   To demonstrate the point-counterpoint dynamic in discussion

- To express curiosity through questioning
- To bring different perspectives to bear on a topic
- To model respectful disagreement
- To express appreciation
- To show comfort with ambiguity

HOW IT WORKS

- A key point about modeling is that it must be publicly explicit. You need to tell people what you're doing and why you're doing it. If your partner asks you a good question don't just say, "That's a good question," and then proceed to answer it. Say why it's a good question (you've never been asked it before, it cuts to the heart of a contradiction in your argument, it introduces a new wrinkle in your thinking, it's beautifully expressed, it extends your thinking, and so on) and let people know that an important part of discussion is relying on others to pose good questions.
- Team members demonstrate how to participate in an ever-expanding organic conversation by making new points, countering or refuting each other's claims, posing alternatives, and striving to see if a synthesis of opposing viewpoints can be developed or what common ground exists.
- Team members demonstrate curiosity and strive to understand other viewpoints by asking questions that invite colleagues to elaborate on their position.
- Team members seek to bring in new perspectives that others are not considering or articulating to make sure whatever is being discussed is considered in its fullest context.
- Team members model respectful disagreement by summarizing a colleagues' viewpoints as accurately as possible to make sure

they have understood them correctly before offering critiques; asking good questions that encourage colleagues to explain the core of their disagreements; giving the fullest reasons possible for disagreements; not seeking to convert colleagues to one's position; changing their minds when appropriate; and remaining open to better arguments or more convincing evidence.

· Team members model living with ambiguity by not always seeking to reach definitive conclusions or neat solutions. A productive discussion can be one in which disagreements and contradictions are clarified and better understood.

WHERE AND WHEN IT WORKS WELL

Team modeling works well in any context. In fact, we think there's a fundamental contradiction when only one of us is in charge of running a workshop, meeting, or class in which we're advocating a discussion-based approach. This is because participants never get to see us doing what we're urging on them: engaging in discussion with peers.

WHAT USERS APPRECIATE

The variety of approaches afforded by team facilitation. Because team members differ in their personalities, identities, and experiences, a higher percentage of participants are likely to feel a connection to the way at least one member of the team operates.

The diversity of perspectives a team brings. Team members working from differing perspectives makes for a more enlivening atmosphere.

The public engagement in disagreement. Nothing gets higher evaluation ratings than when team members disagree strongly yet respectfully with each other. This is theatrically engaging.

The demonstration of *Participation Rubric* indicators. If team members name when they are engaging in specific rubric behaviors and why they consider these to be important, then it helps participants find a way to enact these.

WHAT TO WATCH OUT FOR

Becoming too informal with each other. Teams that have worked together several times, like the two of us, often develop an ease and rapport that comes out as private jokes, muttered asides, and teasing that is off-putting to participants. When we have worked with multicultural groups, we have noticed that some Southeast Asian members are confused when we tease each other, interpreting that as disrespectful.

Agreeing too much. Frequent team teaching can lead to an artificial move to the center where the two or three of you explore only common ground, so you must strive to keep some productive dissonance going.

The discomfort of sitting with profound disagreements. The two of us believe that living with difference is crucial to democratic functioning. But we also know that when we express very different positions people are sometimes left feeling that the workshop, meeting, or class has somehow failed or run aground. So when a session ends with an expression of difference, team members must emphasize to participants that this is valuable in and of itself. They can also commit to exploring and reevaluating those disagreements in future sessions.

QUESTIONS THAT FIT THIS PROTOCOL

Team modeling can be applied to address any question.

CHAPTER 19

Question Brainstorm

Loosely based on the *question formulation technique* developed by Rothstein and Santana (2011), a small group addresses a focus statement by brainstorming as many questions as possible.

PURPOSES

- To give participants practice in developing different kinds of questions
- To develop questions that provide a basis for in-depth study
- To recognize what kinds of questions lead to richer discussion

HOW IT WORKS

- In small groups, participants are presented with a focus statement. Examples are "A learning organization cannot be fully realized without a strong commitment to unfettered discussion" and "Teams that regularly practice discussion are likely to have members who feel empowered."
- Groups brainstorm as many questions as possible suggested by the focus statement. There is no stopping for discussion, judgment, or criticism. Comments are turned into questions whenever possible.
- Questions raised are written down as stated on a blackboard or easel.
- When groups feel they have gone as far as they can with their brainstorming, members begin to erase unpromising questions and underscore those meriting further consideration.
- Concentrating on the underscored questions, groups narrow these down to two or three by asking, "Which questions are most important?" "Which interest us most?" "Which energize us enough to make us want to pursue them further?"
- When groups decide on the two or three best questions, they discuss how to go about responding to them: "What resources would we need?" "What inquiry or research would we need to initiate?" "What discussions would we need to have?"
- The whole gathering convenes, and people reflect on the process.

WHERE AND WHEN IT WORKS WELL

In classrooms, organizations, teams, and communities that have been run on authoritarian, rigid lines. This technique is particularly valuable for settings in which people have not had a lot of opportunities to do creative work.

Situations in which routines, values, and visions have stayed the same. This is a good way to shake up organizations and communities and help them explore future possibilities.

With young people. College and high school students like the concrete guidelines provided and the opportunity to engage in an unrestricted brainstorm.

WHAT USERS APPRECIATE

Brainstorming. This exercise encourages unrestricted, creative thinking, and participants often report how refreshing this is.

The power of questions. Participants like seeing how well-framed questions foster creativity and inquiry.

The feeling of empowerment. When groups exercise control over question posing, they appreciate how this shapes the focus of their discussions.

WHAT TO WATCH OUT FOR

Killing brainstorming with critique. People unfamiliar with brainstorming find it hard to accept and encourage all questions, no matter how off the wall they seem. Emphasize that this exercise is meant to be an opportunity to unleash group creativity and to keep one's inner critic at bay.

Underestimating the value of questions. Finding solutions is culturally and organizationally valued over raising questions. In fact, asking lots of questions is often seen as a diversionary tactic or the exercise of an undisciplined mind. It's important to stress that how questions are framed is crucial for worthwhile discussion.

Premature jettisoning of questions. As groups look over their list of brainstormed questions there will be disagreement about which to keep and which to eliminate. Remind the group not to jettison a question before hearing everyone's view on it.

Confusion about future steps to answer questions. If people are used to having leaders and teachers prescribe how questions should be answered, they will struggle with taking responsibility for developing a plan to answer a group-generated question. You can share examples of how previous groups have done this or demonstrate how you've generated action steps to answer important questions in your own life.

QUESTIONS THAT FIT THIS PROTOCOL

In this case, the focusing statements determine whether worthwhile questions end up being posed. As suggested, provocative and ambitious focus statements provide the best ground for the formulation of interesting and creative questions.

CHAPTER 20

Narrative Listening and Questioning

This exercise uses personal narratives to practice questioning and listening.

PURPOSES

· To practice listening closely and attentively to another person's story
· To use questions to draw out another person's narrative
· To improve people's ability to summarize what was heard in an interaction

HOW IT WORKS

- Two people sit across from one another, with one assuming the role of speaker and the other assuming the role of listener.
- Speakers begin talking about a professional or personal issue that is much on their minds—something they have been thinking a lot about lately.
- Listeners focus only on what the speaker is saying without any thought of how to respond except to show support for the speaker's words.
- Listeners use only questions and perhaps also a supportive or echoing word or two to keep the conversation going. No declarative statements are permitted.
- The speaking with occasional questioning takes five to seven minutes.
- When time is up, listeners briefly summarize what they have heard.
- If necessary, the speaker gently corrects inaccuracies in the listener's summary.
- Roles are then reversed, with the speaker assuming the listener role and the listener assuming the speaker role.
- Participants debrief their reactions to this exercise in the large group.

WHERE AND WHEN IT WORKS WELL

Universality. This is a very simple exercise that works just about everywhere and takes relatively little time. All of us need practice honing our listening skills, and all can use the respectful affirmation of being listened to closely.

As a warm-up. This can be a good warm-up for any gathering devoted to discussion. It helps people get to know each other and reminds everyone that discussion depends on good listening.

WHAT USERS APPRECIATE

The positive experience of being listened to. Speakers invariably comment on how affirming it feels to be listened to so attentively. Close listening brings a group closer together.

The pleasures of listening. Users note that they don't have many opportunities to devote all their psychic and physical energy to listening to another person. This can be both pleasurable and liberating.

WHAT TO WATCH OUT FOR

Not listening. Many of us are not used to listening to someone else without thinking ahead about responding and correcting.

Skipping modeling. Facilitators should demonstrate this protocol ahead of time using a variety of questions, preferably with a team-teaching colleague.

QUESTIONS THAT FIT THIS PROTOCOL

- Questions that provide the prompt for speakers' stories include these:
  - "What's been occupying your mind lately?"
  - "What's going on in your work that feels especially challenging right now?"
  - "If you could be anywhere else right now, where would that be and why?"

- Questions that might be used by listeners in drawing out speakers further include these:
    - "Can you tell me more about that?"
    - "How did that make you feel?"
    - "How did one thing lead to another?"
    - "Why do you think this happened?"
    - "What did you learn from that experience?"

CHAPTER 21

Participation Rubric

Leaders and facilitators typically want good participation in the discussions they convene, but most people assume that participating means talking a lot and sounding smart. When this norm is internalized and unchallenged then the loudest and most confident dominate.

We use versions of the following rubric to interrupt this norm and signal what we mean by good participation. You'll note that none of the behaviors are of the talk-a-lot-and-sound-smart variety.

PURPOSES

· To provide a set of specific behaviors that count as good participation

- To interrupt the expectation that participation is equivalent to talking a lot
- To emphasize that good discussion depends on careful listening and responding
- To create opportunities for introverts and ESL speakers to participate in discussion
- To underscore the importance of synthesizing and building on others' contributions

HOW IT WORKS

Before a discussion-based session, you as facilitator create and distribute a *Participation Rubric* that contains specific examples of what you consider to be good participation:

- Ask a question or make a comment that shows you are interested in what another person says.
- Ask a question or make a comment that encourages another person to elaborate on something he or she has already said.
- Bring in a resource (a reading, web link, video) that adds new information or unexplored perspectives to our learning.
- Post a question, comment, or make a suggestion on *Today's Meet* that takes us in a promising or provocative new direction.
- Make a comment that explicitly underscores the link between two people's contributions.
- Use body language (in only a slightly exaggerated way) to show interest in what different speakers are saying.
- Post a comment on *Today's Meet* (technique 5) that points out an issue we are dodging.
- Make a comment (online if this is appropriate) indicating that you found another person's ideas interesting or useful. Be specific as to why this was the case.

- Contribute something that builds on or springs from what someone else has said. Be explicit about the way you are building on the other person's thoughts—this can be done online.
- Make a comment on your *CIQ* (see technique10) that prompts us to examine discussion dynamics.
- When you think it's appropriate, ask the group for a moment's silence to slow the pace of conversation to give you and others time to think.
- Make a comment that paraphrases at least partly a point someone has already made.
- Make a summary observation that takes into account several people's contributions and that touches on a recurring theme in the discussion (online if you like).
- Ask a cause-and-effect question—for example, "Can you explain why you think it's true that if these things are in place such and such a thing will occur?"
- Find a way to express appreciation for the enlightenment you have gained from the discussion. Try to be specific about what it was that helped you understand something better. Again, this can be done online if you want.

WHERE AND WHEN IT WORKS WELL

This is appropriate for any setting in which you want to signal that good participation depends on listening carefully, asking good questions, synthesizing and connecting points just made, showing appreciation, and drawing others out:

Academic settings. Students in college who are told that they will be graded on class participation as well as academic work need guidance on what this looks like.

Organizational or departmental retreats. We often share an abridged version of this (featuring maybe five items) in the first hour of an organizational retreat.

Program admissions. We have worked in academic programs in which applicants participate in an admissions process requiring them to work together in groups. This is a helpful way to let people know what we're looking for.

WHAT USERS APPRECIATE

The specificity of the indicators. People typically appreciate having highly concrete examples to keep in mind.

Knowing what the leader is looking for. Participants are grateful for knowing exactly what the leader, teacher, or chair means by participation.

The move away from the sounding-smart norm. The emphasis on asking questions, drawing people out, expressing appreciation, and posting online helps remove performance anxiety from those who feel they have to sound smart.

The way indicators build collaboration. Following these indicators builds collaborative patterns of interaction in a group.

WHAT TO WATCH OUT FOR

Indicators that are too restrictive. The previous list gives some examples of indicators we have found helpful, but they are by no means exhaustive. You can adapt these, add to them, and delete any that are unhelpful or unclear. The important point is to give specific indicators to people beforehand of what counts as good participation.

Too many indicators. If the list you provide is too long then people easily can become overwhelmed. Sometimes choosing three or four of them works best for a specific meeting.

The list gets stale. To stop this from becoming predictable, it's often helpful to switch out the items you use so that different indicators are identified at each meeting, workshop, or class.

QUESTIONS SUITED TO THIS TECHNIQUE

This is not a question-generating exercise; however, we have felt it works well in multiple contexts to explain in concrete terms what we mean by good participation. In a sense this rubric is one answer to the question, "What does participation in discussion look like?"

CHAPTER 22

Critical Conversation Protocol

The *Critical Conversation Protocol* is an intensive conversational exercise focused on uncovering the assumptions that inform how someone understands and responds to a seemingly intractable problem. It works best when applied to the analysis of organizational and community problems involving multiple actors.

PURPOSES

· To help someone gain new insights into a problem he or she faces

- To identify and check the assumptions that frame how a problem is perceived
- To present alternative perspectives on a problem that may have been missed
- To suggest specific ways of dealing with intractable problems

HOW IT WORKS

- The protocol involves people playing three conversational roles. The *storyteller* is the person who presents the problem to be examined. The *detectives* are the peers and colleagues who alert the storyteller to assumptions he or she holds about the problem, perspectives that might have been missed, and responses to the problem not previously considered. The *umpire* is the group member who agrees to monitor the conversation by pointing out when people are talking to each other in a judgmental way or contravening the protocol's rules.
- The optimal size for a group using this protocol is eight to twelve members.
- The process begins with the storyteller laying out a problem or situation as he or she sees it by stating what she regards as the facts of the case and the sequence of events involved. This usually takes about ten minutes. The only ground rule here is that interruptions from the detectives are disallowed.
- The detectives then spend ten minutes asking the storyteller questions about the events just described to help them uncover the assumptions they think the storyteller holds. Their questions must request only information to clarify the details of what happened. Detectives should ask only one question at a time. They must refrain from giving their opinions or suggestions, no matter how helpful they feel these might be.

- Examples of judgmental questions would be those beginning with "Did you really believe that…?" "Didn't you think to…?" "Why wouldn't you just…?" "Are you seriously saying…?" "Do you mean to tell us that…?" The umpire points out when she hears these.

- Now the detectives tell the storyteller, on the basis of her story and her responses to their questions, what assumptions they think she holds. The detectives seek to state clearly only what they think the storyteller's assumptions are, not to judge whether they are right or wrong. They are asked to state these assumptions tentatively, descriptively, and nonjudgmentally, using phrases such as "it seems as if…?" "I wonder if one assumption you might be holding is that…?" "Is it possible that you assumed that…?" They state only one assumption at a time and do not give advice. This usually takes five to ten minutes.

- The detectives then give alternative versions of the events that have been described. They are to give these interpretations as descriptions, not judgments. They are describing how others involved in the events might have viewed them, not saying whether or not these perceptions are accurate. Again, no advice is allowed. Again, this typically lasts five to ten minutes.

- The conversation ends with an audit of what's been learned. No ground rules are in place, and detectives can give whatever advice they want (five minutes).

WHERE AND WHEN IT WORKS WELL

When it's demonstrated first by the facilitator. Facilitators should demonstrate how this protocol works by first running through it with the whole workshop, meeting, or community with themselves as storytellers. They present a situation they need help with and have the whole workshop, meeting, or class function as detectives. At each stage of this demonstration facilitators explain the relevant ground rules and respond to participants' questions about it.

When groups have spent time together. We usually keep this exercise in reserve until we feel the groups we have worked with have developed confidence in our leadership and reached a level of trust in their colleagues.

In professional reflection groups. This adapts well to settings in which people are facing problems of practice in their organizations and communities. We have used this with groups as diverse as elementary school and community college teachers, global software corporations, and the military.

If a half-day has been allocated. The initial modeling demonstration takes about an hour, and the smaller groups of eight to twelve conducting the exercise need about fifty minutes. With debriefing, this takes at least half a day.

When participants have relevant experience. This works best if people can draw on their personal histories to ask pointed questions and give good advice.

If work problems are the focus. We have seen storytellers bring highly personal experiences to this exercise ("Should I split up with my partner?"), which puts far too much pressure on the detectives.

WHAT USERS APPRECIATE

Seeing a situation in a new way. Storytellers often learn new ways of thinking about and responding to a problem they thought was beyond them.

Legitimizing personal experience. Even if no new insights emerge, storytellers often feel their experience has been legitimized because detectives confirm the accuracy of the storyteller's assumptions and actions.

Transferring insights. Detectives are often able to apply the insights uncovered and strategies suggested to their own problems.

The focus and structure of the exercise. People often remark on how the specific directions given for the exercise keep it focused on the problem at hand and prevent the discussion going off track.

WHAT TO WATCH OUT FOR

Skipping the modeling. In the interests of time, facilitators may be tempted to skip demonstrating the protocol with the whole community. This is always a mistake. When we have skipped this, we found the small-group application to be much less helpful. So if you can't devote fifty minutes to the demonstration of the process you should not do the exercise.

Time management. It's easy for conversations to get focused on the Q&A section. The umpire or facilitator must try to keep the timing on track.

Premature advice. The great temptation in this exercise is to give advice too early. Detectives want to help by suggesting tips and different approaches right from the start. It's important that the umpire watch out for this and remind everyone that a no-holds-barred, advice-giving session happens at the end of the exercise.

Questions. We have noticed that even experienced practitioners have difficulty formulating questions as a simple request for information. Again, the umpire's role in monitoring this is crucial.

Promising solutions. Although this exercise is meant to alert people to new insights and ways of dealing with problems they face, this won't always happen. Sometimes the problems are too complex for clear solutions to emerge. At other times storytellers have previously analyzed the problem so deeply that detectives have nothing new to add. If this happens, at least the storytellers know that there is nothing that they've missed.

QUESTIONS THAT FIT THIS PROTOCOL

The choice of the problem to be considered is completely in the storyteller's hands, so any topic or situation fits this exercise.

CHAPTER 23

What Are You Hearing?

This technique provides an opportunity for quieter members to check in with the group by repeating or paraphrasing the words others are using.

PURPOSES

· To provide a nonthreatening opportunity for quieter members to participate without having to articulate an idea or take a stand on what has been expressed
· To practice listening and paraphrasing skills

· To identify recurring themes by noting which words and contributions get repeated or paraphrased most

HOW IT WORKS

· The facilitator announces that during the discussion, non-speaking members will be asked periodically to respond to the question, "What are you hearing?" They are told that this is a cue to repeat or paraphrase what others have said.
· As the discussion proceeds, the facilitator models this by summarizing words or phrases.
· When appropriate during the discussion, the facilitator or a member turns to a silent participant and asks, "What are you hearing?" That person is expected to repeat or paraphrase anything that comes to mind.
· The facilitator keeps track of what is said so she can reference them in her *Facilitator Summary* (technique 50) at the end of the discussion.
· As the discussion proceeds, the facilitator notes recurring themes and words identified in response to the question.

WHERE AND WHEN IT WORKS WELL

As a verbal word cloud. What people hear are comments that most attract their attention. Jotting down or typing these words means you can create an electronic word cloud that shows the discussion's recurring themes.

With those unused to discussion. Because participants are not asked to come up with original contributions or synthesize and extend other contributions, this is a nonthreatening way of getting introverts and ESL speakers to participate.

When it's important to hear from everybody. This is a good exercise to try if you as leader really do need to hear from everybody or if participants really do need to learn to speak up in groups.

Its clarity. Unlike more complex discussion protocols, moves, and roles, this is extremely simple. You only need to repeat something that someone else has said.

WHAT USERS APPRECIATE

Being heard. Participants sometimes feel affirmed when their ideas or words are recalled in response to the question.

Valuing listening as a form of participation. Participants who are mostly attentive listeners appreciate having that behavior underscored.

Group GPS. To have someone periodically indicate what is being heard can help a group see the trajectory of the members' discussion more clearly.

Spikes in participation. Because people don't want to be the ones left to paraphrase others' comments, there's sometimes an increase in their participation.

WHAT TO WATCH OUT FOR

Discomfort at being pounced on. Being asked this question can create anxiety and cause people to freeze, so facilitators have to model this first and allow plenty of time for people to respond.

Correcting perceptions. Accept whatever is said as an honest attempt to recall what was heard. Don't tell people they've missed or misheard important themes. It can be quite revealing if someone offers an interpretation that doesn't actually repeat or paraphrase previous comments.

QUESTIONS THAT FIT THIS PROTOCOL

There's only one question for this exercise: "What are you hearing?"

CHAPTER 24

Understanding Check

This exercise asks people to paraphrase a previous speaker's comments to ensure they have accurately understood what they said. When a paraphrase is perceived to be inaccurate, the previous speaker explains what has been misunderstood.

PURPOSES

- To practice active listening
- To practice accurate paraphrasing
- To teach people to check their understandings are accurate

- To demonstrate how easy it is to misinterpret someone's original meaning
- To avoid people attributing words and ideas that speakers did not express

HOW IT WORKS

- Before a discussion everyone agrees to the *Understanding Check* ground rule, which holds that when anyone calls out "check for understanding," the next to speak summarizes the previous speaker's main point and offers a synthesis of the discussion so far before adding something new.
- At any point in the *Understanding Check*, any previous speaker may comment on the accuracy of how well his or her point has been captured.
- Facilitators can model the process early on by asking for a check and then summarizing the speaker's point themselves.
- The group debriefs to see how the exercise went and whether it increased attentiveness to each other's observations.

WHERE AND WHEN IT WORKS WELL

Universality. This has broad applicability to any discussion setting because most people need practice hearing other people's words more accurately.

When participants have developed some familiarity and trust. This works best when a group has experience working together and holds a degree of ease. We avoid using this in the early stages of a group's time together.

When the most powerful in the group are called on. Those who hold most power in an organization or group are sometimes the least likely to take the time to listen to others. This creates an opportunity for them to practice that behavior.

WHAT USERS APPRECIATE

Attention to accuracy. People appreciate others remembering accurately and respectfully what has been said.

Accentuating listening. The pressure on members to report what they have heard accurately leads to closer listening from which everyone benefits.

WHAT TO WATCH OUT FOR

Resistance. Expect some resistance even when group members know each other. People typically want to avoid the tension and anticipatory anxiety this activity produces.

The "gotcha" moment. Participants often feel that at any moment they could be "got" or caught out, so this exercise can feel like an act of aggression. Not knowing when someone will call out "understanding check" creates anxiety, especially if a speaker is then unable to recall or summarize prior comments.

Negative feedback. In the debriefing you will get a lot of feedback that this rule makes participation much more challenging. You will need to remind people that it's designed to improve the ability to listen and to track the group's deliberations.

Skipping modeling. Initially, participants won't request a check for understanding, so early on facilitators should call for checks as often as every four or five minutes and then do the check themselves. This enables participants to see the rule in action.

Not encouraging correcting. Facilitators must keep asking previous speakers if the summaries are accurate. Previous speakers are unlikely to want to correct the summary, particularly if you're doing the summarizing, but you need to keep insisting this happens. This is done best in team facilitation or co-leadership exercises.

Not practicing it enough. Don't just introduce the exercise one week and then drop it the next. Checking for understanding is a helpful practice generally to maintain high levels of attentiveness and keep discussion focused.

QUESTIONS THAT FIT THIS PROTOCOL

Questions that are open-ended and that promote diverse contributions, lively exchanges, and provocative perspectives work best as a basis for practicing close listening. Examples include the following:

· Racial micro-aggressions seem to be everywhere in our organization. Is this a sign of the pervasiveness of racism or of our tendency to exaggerate minor slights?
· How is white supremacy still present in our community?
· Some people believe that sexism remains the world's most pernicious and far-reaching form of bias and prejudice. What are the arguments for this claim? What are the arguments that other forms of bias are even more pervasive?

CHAPTER 25

Stand Where You Stand

We learned this exercise from Joan Naake of Montgomery College in Germantown, Maryland. We like how it teaches people about the complexities of an issue using physical movement and how it opens up the possibility of changing one's mind.

PURPOSES

- To improve participants' ability to develop and articulate arguments
- To invite the possibility of changing one's mind in the face of more convincing arguments or evidence
- To use physical movement to represent changes in thinking

HOW IT WORKS

- The facilitator identifies an issue of importance to a community, class, or organization.
- Before a group meets, participants are asked to read material that provides relevant information on the issue and explores it from different viewpoints.
- When people gather together, the facilitator begins by stating an opinion or making a claim about the issue the group has examined in the prereading.
- Participants spend two to three minutes individually writing down all the reasons why they agree or disagree with the statement just made.
- While people are writing, the facilitator posts four signs around the room reading "strongly agree," "partly agree," "partly disagree," and "strongly disagree."
- When the individual writing time is up, participants are asked to stand underneath the sign that most closely approximates their position on the claim or statement.
- In pairs or trios, people at each station state the reasons for their choice of position.
- People at the different stations then share their reasons for agreeing or disagreeing with the statement to the whole group
- As these arguments are shared, people are free to move to another sign at any time if the arguments they hear convince them to change their position.
- When all four viewpoints have been heard, the group reassesses the numbers of people who support the four positions. Those who have moved during the exercise are asked to share what convinced them to go to a different sign.

- Finally, the whole group assesses which position secures the most agreement, if other information is needed, next steps, and subtleties and nuances revealed.

WHERE AND WHEN IT WORKS WELL

In text-based discussions. This is well suited to academic classes in which students convene for an in-class exploration of the material covered in some prereading.

When organizations are dealing with a new problem or emerging issue. This helps explore alternative approaches and perspectives if no consensus exists.

To encourage open-mindedness. It underscores that changing your mind because of new data or a better argument is a sign of strength, not weakness.

At slow times. This works well when people are getting sleepy—after lunch, at the end of the day, and so on.

WHAT USERS APPRECIATE

Movement. People like to move around the room as a way of expressing the development of their viewpoints. It helps keep energy up during lulls.

Physical representation. It provides a physical representation of how a group's thinking on an issue changes and evolves.

WHAT TO WATCH OUT FOR

One person dominating. Sometimes one person at a station takes too long to give arguments for his or her position. When this happens you have to ask to hear from someone else.

Changing your mind interpreted as weakness or indecision. It helps if you as a facilitator participate in the exercise and move stations a couple of times to show people how you are changing your mind.

All arguments are deemed valid. People are sometimes equally convinced by arguments made at different stations and can't choose one position over another. Remind them that this illustrates how many commitments and beliefs are provisional.

QUESTIONS SUITED TO THIS TECHNIQUE

Stand Where You Stand is suited to finding out where people stand on an issue that affects them either in their community or organization or about course content studied.

CHAPTER 26

Think-Pair-Share

Adapted from Lyman (1981).

This is a buzz group activity in which two or three people briefly share responses to questions and emerging understandings.

PURPOSES

- To get individuals to talk about their developing understandings of a topic
- To bring conversational variety into a learning space
- To use the intimacy of a dyad or triad to increase engagement and understanding
- To focus large-group discussion on issues that matter most to participants

HOW IT WORKS

· During a large-group discussion, lecture, or media presentation, the facilitator asks participants to write down emerging insights or responses to a question.

· These are then shared with one or two people nearby, and each person writes down his or her partner's contributions.

· The discussion, lecture, or media presentation then resumes with people sharing key insights verbally or via *Today's Meet* (technique 5). Alternatively, the dyads or triads can double up to share insights, and the group chooses one to bring back to the large group for further discussion.

WHERE AND WHEN IT WORKS WELL

Universality. *Think-Pair-Share* enjoys something close to universal applicability. It can be done in any organizational, community, or workshop context.

Retaining new knowledge. This exercise helps with retention of material, making it especially appropriate in academe. But it's also useful in town meetings when the details of a new neighborhood plan are being examined, in human resources development trainings to introduce how new legislation affects existing practice, or in organizational rollouts of new strategic plans.

It engages people. It's hard to absorb an uninterrupted flow of information and content. This exercise breaks up that flow. In his meta-review of research on attention spans, Bligh (2000) estimates that about twelve minutes is the maximum time someone can listen attentively to uninterrupted talk and still derive meaning and understanding.

It encourages a deeper level of understanding. Having to talk through your emerging understanding of a new concept or your interpretation of new material helps clarify and deepen understanding.

WHAT USERS APPRECIATE

It's participatory nature. It's energizing to take time out from being a passive recipient of information to think, write, and talk about the content being shared.

Checking in with others. People appreciate having the chance to ask peers a question about material that is difficult or intriguing.

WHAT TO WATCH OUT FOR

Skipping the writing down of insights. It's common to focus on sharing emerging questions and insights only verbally. In our adaptation of *Think-Pair-Share*, writing these down reinforces learning and provides a bridge to later discussions.

Time creep. Remind everyone to be brief when sharing insights and responses in groups because time also must be allocated to bring these back to the whole group.

QUESTIONS THAT FIT THIS PROTOCOL

The kinds of questions that participants might want to share in their pairs and small groups vary widely. Closed questions to check a fact or fill in a blank or open-ended questions of purpose, meaning, and value that have no clear-cut or definitive answers work equally well.

CHAPTER 27

Drawing Discussion

This technique emphasizes visual and graphic ways of talking to each other and is appreciated by those who process information spatially and communicate ideas visually. Even highly word-dependent people like the two of us find it an energizing and refreshing way to deal with familiar questions and topics. We use it to ensure that as wide a variety of participants as possible can feel engaged in a class, workshop, or meeting.

PURPOSES

· To prioritize visual and pictorial expression over spoken and written words

- To free up participants' creative capacities by using symbolic and metaphoric strategies to express ideas
- To enable those who learn best through images and visual representations to exercise leadership
- To add variety and fun to discussion-based interactions

HOW IT WORKS

- A question or problem is posed, such as "What does a good discussion look like?" "How do we know when a theory has explanatory power?" "How can photosynthesis be explained visually?" "What is a moral action?"
- Each participant is given a sheet of paper, a few markers, and a handful of magazines to create a drawing or collage that addresses the question. Highly abstract designs with no attempt at representation are fine. People work by themselves for about ten minutes.
- Participants then convene in small groups, and each person explains his or her drawing or collage to the other group members.
- The group discusses how the individual images connect or contradict each other and works to produce a final group visual incorporating some aspect of each individual's composition. One member takes notes regarding what the group is attempting to communicate.
- Once the group pictures are completed, each is displayed on a wall around the room and a blank sheet of paper is placed next to each.

- People are invited to tour the gallery of visuals and provide comments, questions, and reactions on the blank sheets. They are encouraged to do this using images rather than words.
- The whole group reconvenes, and participants can ask different groups about their postings. The member who took notes as the group visual was developed takes the lead in responding to questions posed about a group's drawing or collage.

WHERE AND WHEN IT WORKS WELL

In highly verbal environments. This is a refreshing change in settings where there's a strong and habitual reliance on the spoken and written word.

To express the inexpressible. This offers a creative way for members to communicate ideas and feelings that are expressed more powerfully visually.

Relationship building. The energy of this technique often gets people to relate to each other more casually and amiably.

WHAT USERS APPRECIATE

The change of pace. The routine of PowerPoint presentations, Q&A, small-group discussions, and large-group debriefings is dramatically interrupted by this exercise.

The chance to exercise creativity. *Drawing Discussion* is an opportunity to flex creative muscles and explore issues with new freedom and intellectual abandon.

The raised energy of enjoyment. The move away from traditional communication formats inevitably raises the level of energy in the room. We like to do this in the afternoons and evenings when flatness and sameness set in.

WHAT TO WATCH OUT FOR

Pacing. Facilitators must be on the lookout for groups that are unusually speedy and those that are surprisingly unhurried. Some groups finish up prematurely and should be encouraged to add more content and depth to their postings. Others are reluctant to move from the discussion to the drawing part of the exercise or tend to linger over unnecessary pictorial details. They should be reminded to stay within the agreed-on time limits.

Abstractness. The drawings really get groups' creative juices flowing, but sometimes this also means that the representations they produce are highly abstract and difficult to understand or interpret. This is why the note-taker role is crucial for the final debriefing.

Self-consciousness. Both of us are like many others who feel they have no artistic, drawing, or graphic ability. Facilitators must keep reminding everyone that artistic proficiency is irrelevant and that abstract images are encouraged.

Modeling. Facilitators should participate in the exercise by creating their own visuals. If they have no artistic ability, this underscores their commitment to the exercise.

Mistiming the introduction of the exercise. This is best introduced when you have already built some credibility and trust with the group. In a highly formal or authoritarian setting, people will typically initially recoil from something as flaky as a drawing or collaging discussion. Facilitators should emphasize it's a good way to loosen up people and uncover previously unarticulated ideas and viewpoints.

QUESTIONS THAT FIT THIS PROTOCOL

- Questions that fit being answered in visual terms obviously work well here: "What does it look like when a meeting or discussion is sabotaged?" "What would it look like for our community to be effective?" "What does effective collaboration across our organization look like?"
- Questions that ask for actions or behaviors also work well: "How do leaders behave who support their coworkers in performing their best work?" "How can we get people in the community more involved in local initiatives?"

CHAPTER 28

Musicalizing Discussion

This is another way to energize workshops, meetings, trainings, and classes that are getting stale. Participants use kazoos, tambourines, and voice to demonstrate musically the patterns of their discussions or to capture the dynamics of a problem.

PURPOSES

- To bring variety and zest to formats that are getting stale from routine
- To unleash creative impulses in enacting discussion dynamics
- To use nonverbal means to explain and shed light on a familiar experience

HOW IT WORKS

- Small groups of six to eight members are given kazoos, tambourines, and triangles so everyone has an instrument.
- The assignment is to create a musical composition of up to a minute that uses instruments and voices to capture the dynamics of a problem, issue, or experience.
- Members are told to keep in mind the possibilities of creating these choices in their music:
  - Moments of harmony and dissonance
  - Periods of silence, loudness, crescendo, and decrescendo
  - Solos interspersed with ensemble playing
  - Variations on a theme
  - Different musical sounds connecting and responding to each other
  - Conflict that may or may not be resolved harmonically
  - Compositions that emphasize balance and symmetry
  - Compositions that emphasize chaos and disorder
- Facilitators briefly demonstrate how they might musicalize some of the dynamics above to represent their understanding of a specific topic.
- Groups disperse for about twenty minutes to create their compositions.
- When ready, groups return, and each performs its composition.
- The whole group reconvenes to discuss what different compositions conveyed and any new insights that were gained as a result.

WHERE AND WHEN IT WORKS WELL

In a one- or two-day workshop. The technique is not particularly time consuming and can infuse energy into a brief workshop.

To build community. This activity helps people let their hair down and get to know one another in a more relaxed and personal way.

With creative arts organizations. Not surprisingly, this technique often works well with groups sharing a creative or artistic orientation, such as a community theatre, community arts organization, or museum.

Where institutional routines have become stale. Groups that meet many times over a period of weeks or months are likely to benefit from an exercise that infuses their interactions with new energy. This technique can be a lot of fun and unleash group members' creativity.

WHAT USERS APPRECIATE

Affirming different ways of knowing. Many participants, especially musicians and other artists, appreciate the recognition that communicating through music is a way to make sense of the world.

Relationship building. Musicalizing enables participants to interact more informally and to develop relationships.

Unleashing creativity. It frees people up to try out new ideas and communicate in a new way.

It's energizing. People like the way it introduces energy into a formal setting.

WHAT TO WATCH OUT FOR

Discomfort. Many find this uncomfortable and disorienting, so facilitators need to acknowledge this. They should stress how using an unfamiliar medium to express understanding often results in new insights.

151

Confusion. Participants usually need help, at least at first, figuring out what it means to musicalize discussion. Showing video streams of previous group attempts is often helpful.

Making sure you model the exercise. Facilitators should model how they might musicalize their analyses of problems, providing lots of concrete examples people can build on.

Time constraints. Make sure to give the full twenty minutes for creating the composition and ten minutes to discuss any new insights that occurred.

QUESTIONS THAT FIT THIS PROTOCOL

· "How does it feel to be made to implement actions you don't agree with?"
· "What does our communication sound like?"
· "What makes for an effective team?"
· "What does a discussion sound like that is a mix of strong agreement and strong disagreement?"
· "How do we live our mission?"
· "What does it sound like to be fulfilled in your work?"
· "How do we deal with setbacks and frustrations to our cause?"

CHAPTER 29

Structured Silence

A crucial element in a conversational rhythm is silence. Yet lulls in a discussion are often experienced as awkward and interpreted to mean that nothing is happening. *Structured Silence* is a way to help people become comfortable with silence as an integral part of any discussion session.

PURPOSES

- To embed periods of silence in discussions so that participants feel comfortable during these lulls
- To keep discussion grounded and focused by introducing regular opportunities for people to identify important points and new questions
- To give those who have not contributed an opportunity to shape the conversation

HOW IT WORKS

- Every fifteen minutes or so the facilitator asks people to pause for two to three minutes to think about a question that they or another person has posed.
- Examples of questions we often ask are "What's the most important point that's been made so far today?" "What questions have been raised for you in the discussion up to now?" "Which of your assumptions about the topic have been confirmed and which have been challenged in the last twenty minutes?" "What important perspectives are we missing?" "What's so confusing or puzzling that we need to revisit it?"
- During this pause, participants write down their responses to the question on 3' × 5' cards. Alternatively, they post their thoughts on *Today's Meet* (technique 5). Facilitators stress this is anonymous.
- After two or three minutes people pass their cards to the facilitator, who chooses several comments at random and shares these with the group. Alternatively, facilitators can pull up the *Today's Meet* feed on the screen and invite people to comment on any responses that intrigue them.
- Based on participant responses, the facilitator and group talk about where the discussion should go next.

WHERE AND WHEN IT WORKS WELL

With quieter, more hesitant groups. People's natural silence is acknowledged as an important part of the discussion.
With groups who tend to veer off in multiple directions. This helps a group stay focused on exploring the question at hand and deepening the discussion.

154

With hierarchical groups. This is a good way to encourage contributions if a clear hierarchy exists in the group and quieter members are intimidated about saying something critical or suggesting a new direction.

WHAT USERS APPRECIATE

Anonymity. Conducted properly, this exercise enables people to ask difficult questions, critique the leader, or admit to confusion without being identified.

It equalizes participation. Introverts and ESL speakers appreciate the chance to shape the course of the discussion.

It grounds discussion. Participants report that stopping regularly to respond to a question helps keep the conversation focused on the topic.

Discussion develops organically. Instead of veering from one topic to the other, the conversation builds in an organic way, with regular references back to earlier comments and contributions.

WHAT TO WATCH OUT FOR

Discomfort with silence. The first couple of times you do this, you can play some quiet background instrumental music so that there is not total silence.

Mistiming the silent pause. Sometimes a discussion is going so well that interrupting it with this exercise causes a loss of momentum and energy. At other times a crucial moment in a discussion is reached when people are grappling with a difficult issue or confronting a contradiction, so don't do this rigidly every fifteen minutes. Use your best judgment and ignore it when necessary.

QUESTIONS THAT FIT THIS PROTOCOL

Take note of the questions we often ask as prompts for *Structured Silence* in the "How It Works" section:

- "What's the most important point that's been made so far today?"
- "What questions have been raised for you in the discussion up to now?"
- "Which of your assumptions about the topic have been confirmed and which have been challenged in the last twenty minutes?"
- "What important perspectives are we missing?"
- "What's so confusing or puzzling that we need to revisit it?"

CHAPTER 30

Writing Discussion

This technique draws on the advantages of online discussion boards and chat rooms and transfers them to live, face-to-face discussion settings. In small groups, participants respond to a question or problem through texting, instant messaging, or handwriting in block letters on notecards. A debrief reflects on its strengths and weaknesses.

PURPOSES

- To experience relating to others who may or may not be physically present solely through written, not oral, communication
- To support those who find the fast pace of oral discussion unnerving and who prefer a more deliberative style of written communication

· To combine written communication with eye contact, gesturing, body language, and touch

HOW IT WORKS

· In small groups of five people consider a question or problem. Participants are told that written communication is the primary mode. No speech is permitted. Participants are also encouraged to use facial cues and body language to amplify their written communication.
· In live meetings, workshops, and classes people handwrite messages on notecards. Each person writes in big enough letters for everyone in the group to see, and the notecards are placed in the center of the table or pinned to an easel. Now everyone can see all of them as the discussion proceeds, and they can be moved to accommodate new postings or be rearranged into new clusters.
· In a spoken debrief, members talk about the advantages and disadvantages of relying on written communication.

WHERE AND WHEN IT WORKS WELL

Online discussion boards. The inspiration for this technique arises from discussion boards in which almost all communication occurs through writing. This technique is thus especially appropriate, even necessary, in online settings.

When you want to deemphasize speech. Those who are not comfortable relying solely on the spoken word appreciate even a temporary shift to the written word.

To deepen discussion. In contrast to the transitory nature of speech, writing sometimes enables people to probe a topic more comprehensively.

WHAT USERS APPRECIATE

It's easier to keep track of the discussion. People can review all the preceding contributions before making a comment.

It enables time to process information. Those who need time to ponder questions are often drawn to this activity.

Introverts are more relaxed. Removing the pressure to speak extemporaneously is a big relief to introverts.

WHAT TO WATCH OUT FOR

The frustration of garrulous extroverts. Confining their comments to writing often frustrates extroverts. Remind people there will always be those who appreciate slowing down the discussion and using the more deliberative approach of writing.

Neglecting texting. A discussion using texting that is projected onto a screen (perhaps on *Today's Meet* or *Backchannel Chat*) is different from one using notecards. Younger students typically prefer to text.

The loss of spontaneity and camaraderie. In a live spoken discussion you can sometimes feel the energy crackling in the room as people excitedly finish each other's sentences, jump in with examples, and respond immediately. This energy is less evident in *Writing Discussion* but is replaced by a more reflective tone.

Failing energy. In the age of the keyboard, lengthy discussion relying entirely on handwritten messages can quickly get tiring and frustrating. Bring the exercise to a close if it is causing special difficulty for participants.

Illiteracy. Note the caveat we offered regarding *Quick Writes*. This is potentially humiliating when people are not literate or not comfortable writing.

Dyslexia and spelling difficulties. Those with dyslexia or who have spelling difficulties will find this uncomfortable.

QUESTIONS THAT FIT THIS PROTOCOL

Because this technique focuses on a method of communication, there are no specific questions associated with it.

CHAPTER 31

Quick Writes

Quick Writes takes two to three minutes and is intended to remove some of the performance anxiety people feel at speaking extemporaneously.

PURPOSES

- To get people immediately focused on a question or issue
- To write down thoughts so that participants have something to contribute
- To remove some of the anxiety associated with speaking extemporaneously
- To provide an opening for text-based discussions

HOW IT WORKS

· Participants write a response to a question or prompt about their prior reading of a text such as a report, policy brief, program evaluation, or assigned chapter.

· People have two to three minutes to write their answers as extensively as possible (sometimes called *free writes*). They keep these for the group discussion.

· Quick writes are then used in a variety of ways in the whole-group conversation. They can be read verbatim in whole or in part, provide prompts for new comments, or be cited as thoughts that get revised as discussion proceeds.

WHERE AND WHEN IT WORKS WELL

When people are unused to discussion. *Quick Writes* works especially well with new discussion participants who appreciate the time to think through and write out their contribution.

When participants are reluctant to offer a comment. Reading a response often makes people less anxious about contributing to a discussion.

In situations when it is important to complete prior reading. Participants are more likely to complete prior reading when they know the reading will be the basis for an opening quick write.

When people prefer to express themselves in writing. Many people are more comfortable writing out their thoughts about a text, at least initially. This exercise lets them work from their strengths.

WHAT USERS APPRECIATE

Writing before speaking. Many people tell us that they think and speak more clearly about a topic when they write their thoughts down first.

Deepens reflections. Some participants say discussion goes deeper when it begins with written reflections.

WHAT TO WATCH OUT FOR

Finding the right place to contribute. For many participants it's difficult to find the right place to read out a quick write. They have to wait until the communicative traffic is relatively light to squeeze their comment in. Facilitators can help by regularly asking groups "Are there any *Quick Writes* that seem to speak to this issue? Let's hear them."

Someone else has said your comment. Sometimes a member's *Quick Write* is similar to one already spoken. If that's the case, it's hard to articulate it without seeming redundant.

Illiteracy. Doing this in any setting in which some participants may be illiterate can be devastating and lead to unnecessary shame and humiliation. If you don't know the literacy status of potential participants, this technique can put disempowered people into an even more subordinate position.

QUESTIONS THAT FIT THIS PROTOCOL

· "What are the most important ideas from this presentation for you and why?"

- "What are key lessons from this text and how might you use them in your life?"
- "How would you summarize this conversation for a friend who wasn't here?"
- "Where do we need to go next in dealing with this problem?"

CHAPTER 32

Cocktail Party

The *Cocktail Party* is an informal technique meant to loosen people up and get them to think about a question in a new way. It often amuses and even astonishes people who aren't expecting it. So if you want to startle people into processing a question differently, this could be the right tool.

PURPOSES

- To infuse new enthusiasm into discussion through a diverting, unorthodox, and yet familiar form of interaction
- To gather a wide variety of views about a question or topic
- To shake up thinking and provoke creative responses to a question or topic

HOW IT WORKS

- Facilitators prepare hors d'oeuvres and nonalcoholic drinks before the class, meeting, or training. On 3' × 5' cards they write conversation prompts meant to stimulate new thinking about the question or issue being considered and place two or three of the cards on each tray.
- Facilitators announce that today's discussion will be modeled on a cocktail party and that people will mingle with others to discuss their responses to a question or problem that is posed to the group.
- Facilitators serve conversation prompts, as well as food and drink, from trays they carry around the meeting room.
- Participants are urged to move around the room and to talk to and hear from as many people as possible. They eat, drink, chat, and mingle, discussing the various prompts they are served. People are asked to start a new conversation with a new person or a different small group about every five minutes.
- Finally, the whole group reconvenes and individuals share the variety of viewpoints they heard as they made their way around the room.

WHERE AND WHEN IT WORKS WELL

Higher education. One group that has responded quite favorably to the *Cocktail Party* is college students, mainly because it takes them by surprise to have drinks served to them by the teacher-waiter! When the goal is to boost engagement or set a more positive tone, the *Cocktail Party* can be a nice way to get there. **Staff development.** Mandatory staff development is often anticipated with dread. The assumption is that "experts" will talk from PowerPoints about something people don't really need to know and can't use. The novelty of this exercise engages people immediately.

WHAT USERS APPRECIATE

Playfulness. People tell us this activity is refreshing and liberating. Consequently, it livens things up, giving participants license to say things, offer critiques, and generate ideas that might not otherwise be expressed.

Informality. Many note how refreshing it is to speak with others under such relaxed conditions.

WHAT TO WATCH OUT FOR

Keeping people on task. Because of its looseness and informality, this exercise is especially tangent prone. As you wander the room you can ask a refocusing question if things seem to be drifting.

Getting people to mingle. Similar to any party, people tend to get deep into discussion knots with one or two other guests. Make sure you invite participants to switch to a new partner or group every five minutes or so.

QUESTIONS THAT FIT THIS PROTOCOL

The questions that work best are those that are broad and encourage diverse viewpoints:

- "What's the most memorable moment you've experienced since you joined this organization?"
- "What makes you disengage from a meeting?"
- "What things have we done that work especially well?"

CHAPTER 33

Bohmian Dialogue

Based on David Bohm's *On Dialogue* (1996), this technique is a process for getting groups to talk and think together more deeply and coherently.

PURPOSES

- To create a flow of meaning among dialogue participants
- To think more effectively together
- To build on one another's ideas creatively and freely
- To identify what gets in the way of shared meaning and collective thought
- To think productively about seemingly intractable problems

HOW IT WORKS

- Participants form into a circle and the convener explains the meaning of dialogue: there are no winners or losers and no attempt to persuade, the focus is on understanding what people actually say without judgment or criticism, and the object is to develop collective thinking.
- Bohm recommends talking about dialogue itself when people first come together through questions such as "What makes dialogue so difficult?" or "What conditions foster good dialogue?"
- There is no pressure to respond to the question immediately. People are encouraged to be silent and to speak only when they have a thought prompted by another's comment. Silence indicates people are actually thinking. If it's helpful, participants are encouraged to close their eyes or look at the floor.
- This process continues for as long as seems optimal. Bohm recommends two hours but we sometimes use much briefer chunks of fifteen to thirty minutes.
- The process concludes with participants sharing what they came to understand more deeply.

WHERE AND WHEN IT WORKS WELL

When sufficient time is allotted. People need enough deliberative time to see noteworthy results.

In settings that value contemplative deliberation. We have seen this work well in congregations, self-help groups, seminaries, and higher education. However, corporations looking for new and better ways to lead their organizations were early adopters.

To break hierarchical patterns. Community groups trying to democratize their interactions find this useful.

WHAT USERS APPRECIATE

How powerful it can be. It's revealing and refreshing to participate in this process.

The valuing of participants. Each person's contribution to the whole is explicitly appreciated.

The absence of competition and one-upmanship. The process bypasses the temptation to rebut or proselytize.

The experience of authentic collective thinking. New directions and possibilities sometimes emerge from this way of talking and thinking together.

WHAT TO WATCH OUT FOR

Initial frustration and hostility about the process. Frustration at the lack of structure is normal and to be expected. Don't stop it from being expressed but don't back down. This looseness helps release imaginative thinking and foster careful listening.

Time constraints. Give it enough time and don't expect too much if you don't.

The group size. Bohm (1996) recommends forty members so the group represents the diversity of experience and opinion that often undermines dialogue. We have easily adapted this process to smaller groups.

QUESTIONS THAT FIT THIS PROTOCOL

· "What makes dialogue so difficult?"
· "What conditions foster good dialogue?"
· "What's stopping us realizing our potential?"
· "What do we need to do our best work?"
· "What do we do best?"

CHAPTER 34

Methodological Belief

Trying to understand the logic and rationale informing a viewpoint very different from our own is one of the hardest intellectual and emotional leaps to make in discussion. We find that people are more open to it if it is done in short five-minute bursts.

PURPOSES

- To practice being disciplined believers to supplement our considerably greater experience as disciplined doubters
- To experience the "virtues and strengths" (Elbow, 1986, p. 257) of asserting belief in an unfamiliar viewpoint

- To open participants to the possibility of changing fixed perceptions
- To explore how shared beliefs can build community

HOW IT WORKS

- The exercise begins with observing methodological belief in action. We usually use an example from the film *Color of Fear* in which a white man who has persistently doubted the existence of racism is asked, "What's keeping you from believing that life for people of color is really that harsh, cruel, and pervasive?" The answer—"You wouldn't want to think that people can be that mean toward one another"—is followed up by another question: "What if they really are?" The clip ends with the response "That's a tragedy."
- This example is discussed as an example of methodological belief in which the white man sheds his habit of doubting and affirms, however briefly, that racism might be as pervasive and cruel as he has been told.
- The facilitator then proposes a question-statement as something for people to believe in. Examples might be as follows:
  - "The most effective organizations depend chiefly on the quality of questions people ask. Assuming this is true, how should our organization change?"
  - "Racial micro-aggressions pervade our community's processes. Assuming this is true, what do we need to do?"
- Small groups are given five minutes to brainstorm their responses and then the whole workshop, class, or meeting convenes to share their responses. People are asked particularly to share new insights and ways their views have changed.

174

WHERE AND WHEN IT WORKS WELL

Team building. Practicing methodological belief helps instill an awareness and appreciation of the different talents and perspectives of team members.

Guarding against groupthink. Even the most critically alert groups sometimes move too quickly to an assumed consensus. This technique stretches to consider alternative perspectives and possibilities.

When introducing a challenging idea or practice. The five-minute time limit means participants will consider challenging ideas knowing it's only for a brief period.

Creating an inclusive environment. When genuine and serious differences of experience and perspectives exist, this technique helps people feel their views are being taken seriously.

WHAT USERS APPRECIATE

Entertaining alternative viewpoints. Many people enjoy the creativity of briefly exploring new and alternative points of view as if they were true.

A worthy challenge. Trying to affirm a perspective they don't agree with is something that many participants find bracing.

Changing minds. It doesn't happen often, but a few participants have appreciated the change in mind-set that has come about as a result of this exercise.

WHAT TO WATCH OUT FOR

The artificiality of playacting. Asking people to act for five minutes as if they believe something unfamiliar is true is sometimes experienced as a waste of time. You need to remind people that striving for intersubjective understanding (Habermas, 1984) or perspective taking (Mezirow, 1991) is necessary to the kind of consensus building or conflict resolution that can move projects forward.

The difficulty of mental stretching. It's extremely hard to believe in a perspective or statement that challenges some of your axiomatic assumptions and even harder to imagine what things would be like if a statement you disagree with is actually true, so crafting a belief statement that provokes and unleashes creativity is crucial.

The potential for abuse. A situation could arise in which participants are asked to believe in some frightening things such as "Racism does not exist and is entirely in the minds of people of color" or "Indigenous people have no right to their ancestral lands" or "Climate change is a liberal hoax entirely unsupported by evidence." Even devoting just five minutes to believing in such statements can strengthen bigotry and divisiveness.

QUESTIONS THAT FIT THIS PROTOCOL

Here are some questions and what-if situations that we have found useful:

- "What if racism is as cruel, harsh, and pervasive as people of color say it is?"
- "What would it mean for us if feeling appreciated were the strongest motivator for working hard?"
- "What if the quality of questions we ask determines how effective our organizations and communities are?"
- "What if the thing that makes the biggest difference for how employees feel about their supervisors is the level of respect they receive from them?"

CHAPTER 35

Justifiable Pressure

Similar to Baptiste (2000) we believe there is such a thing as ethical coercion: using your authority to force someone to do something he or she doesn't want to do because you judge it's in their best interests. In the case of discussion, we know that unless those unused to speaking participate early on in a series of meetings, the chances that they will say anything falls precipitously as time goes by, so sometimes we have to pressure people to speak up so they know their voices will be heard.

PURPOSES

- To get usually silent participants used to contributing to a discussion
- To provide a range of safe ways to get people over the anxiety of speaking for the first time

HOW IT WORKS

To make justifiable pressure work, it's important not to spring it on people. At the start of a discussion facilitators announce they'll be using a range of techniques to get everybody to participate, such as the following:

- **Pass and return.** If people decline to speak, let them know you'll return to them in a few minutes for a response to the same question.
- **Extend wait time.** Allow people time to respond, up to maybe thirty seconds. The first few times this happens there will be a tension or embarrassment but after a while people become more comfortable with this dynamic.
- **Online posting.** Allow the option of not speaking when called but require that a response be posted online by the end of the day. Then check, and if it's not there remind the person (publicly) that their comment is expected.
- **Social media *Quick Write*.** Tell discussants to post on *Today's Meet* (technique 5) and then check the feed for their comment every ten to fifteen minutes.
- **Alternate week arrangement.** One week you will call on people; the next you won't.
- **Justifying the request.** When asking someone to speak, you explain why you'd like to hear from that person (they have relevant experience, they posted something interesting online, something they said outside the session caught your attention, etc.).
- **Reasons for reluctance.** Ask speakers why they find it difficult to respond. Sometimes you find your question is unclear or that you've misunderstood the group's previous knowledge.

· **Asking silent participants.** Tell the group, "Now I'd like to hear responses to this question only from people who haven't had a chance to speak yet."

WHERE AND WHEN IT'S WORKED WELL

When people trust the facilitator. If people judge you're doing this to encourage participation rather than to embarrass them they're more likely to respond so introduce these only after you've worked with a group for some time.

When there is team facilitation. This works best if a team has modeled using these approaches with each other in front of a workshop, class, or meeting.

WHAT USERS APPRECIATE

Being heard. Although initially discomfiting, people tell us that in the long run they are glad finally to have their contribution acknowledged.

Time allowed. People appreciate being able to return back to them, which deliberately allows time to think before contributing.

Negotiation. People appreciate a give-and-take between leader and participants such as alternating which week you call on them.

WHAT TO WATCH OUT FOR

Hectoring. If you're not careful you can seem to be blaming or hectoring.

Embarrassing participants. If thirty seconds of wait time goes by without a response, this can embarrass participants as everyone sits in awkward silence.

179

Justifiable resistance. Just as there is justifiable pressure there is also justifiable resistance to speaking. Be open to the possibility that you're exerting pressure in an irresponsible way.

Mistiming. If you haven't earned the right to ask people to respond or if they're suspicious of you or the setting, then your pressure will likely backfire.

Difficulty of modeling. If you are running a discussion alone it's unwieldy to try to model these approaches by asking yourself a question and then allowing wait time for you to answer, saying why you can't respond, and so on.

QUESTIONS THAT FIT THESE PROTOCOLS

The specific questions you invite previously silent participants to respond to will arise naturally from the discussion.

CHAPTER 36

Hatful of Quotes

In discussions based on previously assigned reading material—say the draft of an organizational strategic plan or an academic text reviewing theory or new content—people are often reluctant to contribute. They don't want to show themselves up by responding in the wrong way, highlighting irrelevant points, or demonstrating fundamental misunderstandings. *Hatful of Quotes* is designed to ease the anxiety of having to sound smart while ensuring that discussion is grounded in the text.

PURPOSES

· To keep participants focused on discussing the actual text that has been assigned

- To ease the pressure of impromptu discussion or calling on people for a response
- To allow time for those who need to think before speaking
- To remove the performance anxiety of having to demonstrate full and accurate command of the text

HOW IT WORKS

- Prior to a discussion of a text, the facilitator types out key sentences, recommendations, or contentious assertions from the document studied. Each quote is typed multiple times onto separate slips of paper.
- These quotes are placed in a hat or bowl and in the meeting, workshop, or class the facilitator asks participants to draw out one of the slips of paper.
- People take up to a minute to think about the quote they've picked and then everyone is asked to read out their quote and comment on it. The order of contribution is up to the participants.
- Those who feel more fearful about speaking typically go last. Because the same five or six quotes are used, those who go later will have heard their quote read out and commented on by those who spoke earlier, so even if they have little to say about their own interpretation of the quote, they can affirm, build on, or contradict a comment a peer has already made on that quote.
- When everyone has responded the group moves into open discussion.

WHEN AND WHERE IT WORKS WELL

Text-based discussions. This technique is obviously meant for situations in which participants have been assigned prereading and the discussion is intended to explore reactions to the assigned text.

When focusing on contentious ideas. Sometimes people wish to avoid controversial or difficult parts of a text. Selecting certain quotes ensures that people don't duck contentious issues or complex ideas.

WHAT USERS APPRECIATE

The time to think. Shy, introverted, or ESL speakers can think about what they wish to say or write it down before speaking.

The focus on a specific excerpt from the text. Being asked to respond to a specific quote focuses attention in a more helpful way than asking, "What strikes you most about the text?" For some this question is too obtuse and confusing.

The scaffolding provided by earlier responses. For those unable to respond initially to a quote it's helpful to hear other people's responses. These often trigger a reaction, question, or additional thought about the original comment.

How participation is democratized. Everyone gets to speak but in a way that is safer than in many open discussions.

WHAT TO WATCH OUT FOR

Ditto. The most diffident or reluctant students will often say, "I agree with Lyron or Eva" when their turn arrives. Let people know you might ask follow-up questions to elaborate on their responses so this doesn't take them by surprise.

The usual suspects. The most voluble and confident usually go first, which tends to reinforce the pecking order already established in the group. If this keeps happening you can choose the first two or three people to respond.

QUESTIONS SUITED TO THIS TECHNIQUE

Because this technique involves the facilitator choosing the quotes and excerpts, the use of specific questions is not really applicable.

CHAPTER 37

Quotes to Affirm and Challenge

Discussions based on preassigned reading are some of the hardest to facilitate. Some participants only skim the reading; others ignore it entirely or come determined to talk only about one idea that captures their attention. When the conversation opens, it quickly becomes an exchange of generalizations and platitudes with claims attributed to the text that stand unchecked. This technique is intended to address these problems.

PURPOSES

· To ensure everyone reads the material beforehand
· To keep the discussion focused on the text

- To prevent inaccurate attributions
- To reveal similarities and differences in how people respond to a reading
- To highlight parts of the text that were most resonant or dissonant for readers

HOW IT WORKS

- When participants are asked to read preassigned material they are each told to bring to the meeting one quote from the reading they wish to affirm and one they wish to challenge.
- The quote to affirm could be chosen because it's thought to be empirically accurate or it tallies with someone's experience. Maybe it represents the most important point or the kernel of the argument. Perhaps it's lyrically rousing or rhetorically powerful.
- The quote to challenge could be chosen because it's inaccurate or incomprehensible. Maybe it's contradicted by experience or advocating something reprehensible or immoral.
- When the meeting is convened people are put in small groups of five. Each person shares the quotes he or she has affirmed and challenged and the reasons they were chosen.
- After discussion the small group chooses one quote to affirm and one to challenge out of all the quotes proposed. Sometimes the quote is chosen because more than one person proposes it. Sometimes it's chosen because it provokes the most discussion or the reasoning behind one person's choice persuades other members. The two quotes must come from different members of the small group.
- The quotes are posted around the room on sheets of newsprint together with a summary of the reasons for the group's choices. A blank sheet is posted next to each poster.

186

- Participants are given markers and asked to wander the room individually and post their support for or objections to the quotes they read.
- The small groups then gather at their original posting to read and discuss the comments others have left. After a few minutes the whole group reconvenes to consider which quotes seem pivotal and which generated the most reaction.

WHEN AND WHERE IT WORKS WELL

Text-based discussions. This technique is obviously designed for situations in which participants have been assigned prereading beforehand and the discussion is intended to explore people's reactions.

When people are intimidated by reading large amounts of text. The requirement to choose only two quotes to talk about is much less daunting than being asked to respond to global questions such as "What reactions did the reading provoke?"

In academic settings. This is a good technique when instructors teach specific course content and wish to elicit the meanings students ascribe to a text.

Town hall meetings. This works for a task force meeting considering a new strategic plan, a town hall meeting reviewing the findings of an environmental impact study, or any group faced with a document that affects their operations.

WHAT USERS APPRECIATE

The diversity of responses. When a range of quotes are proposed, participants are often surprised to find out how people have read the same words differently.

Everyone participates. In the small-group stage, all members have the chance to propose and defend their quotes.

The discussion goes deeper into the text. In both the small and large groups, people constantly flick through the assigned text to read specific sentences and paragraphs.

The time spent reading the text beforehand is justified. People feel that time spent on the assigned reading has been worthwhile.

WHAT TO WATCH OUT FOR

Small groups are at loggerheads about which quotes to choose. In this case suggest that the two quotes chosen represent the different positions existing in the group.

Too great a diversity of quotes is proposed. Sometimes there seems to be no common ground or meeting point suggested by the range of different quotes posted around the room. But this in itself is revealing. It stops people from universalizing their own response to the reading and helps them understand that a variety of different positions are in the room.

Reasons not provided. Small groups often focus so much on the meaning of the quotes they've chosen that they neglect to document the reasons behind their choices. Remind them shortly before posting that these need to be included.

QUESTIONS SUITED TO THIS TECHNIQUE

This focuses on responding to texts rather than raising questions.

CHAPTER 38

Jigsaw

When a topic can be broken down easily into different components participants can become familiar with one specific and then teach others about it.

PURPOSES

- To show how discussion can be used to develop group expertise on a topic
- To invite participants to become experts by teaching topics to each other
- To experience two very different discussion dynamics—one in which people learn together and one in which they teach each other

HOW IT WORKS

- A relatively large group decides to study a topic that lends itself to being broken down into five or six subtopics.
- Small groups of five or six form around each subtopic. The number of participants in each group should be the same as the number of subtopics.
- In the first "expert" round, each small group chooses a different subtopic and each member agrees to read up on that topic.
- The small groups reconvene after a period and share what they have learned. They raise questions about the topic, explore common understandings, identify disagreements, and consider different interpretations.
- The small group members summarize what they have all come to know about their assigned subtopic and decide on the key points they wish to share and some strategies on how they might teach these in the next round.
- The second round begins as new groups form comprising one expert representative from each of the original subtopic areas.
- Each expert takes responsibility for sharing key findings and important questions regarding his or her subtopic.
- After a suitable time the whole group is convened to discuss lessons learned, enduring questions, and future directions.

WHERE AND WHEN IT WORKS WELL

Leadership development. *Jigsaw* provides the chance for participants to experience leadership in bite-sized chunks. For a short period they are responsible for helping others develop skill and knowledge.

190

Enhancing division of labor. It works well in teams in which a number of tasks need to be accomplished and there are limited resources for their completion.

Deepening learning in academic settings. This technique encourages closer reading and research because students have to become experts on a subtopic.

WHAT USERS APPRECIATE

It promotes collaboration. People practice cooperation that builds more cohesive teams.

Control over learning. People know the learning that occurs stems entirely from their own efforts.

Having expertise acknowledged. Each expert appreciates being seen as the resource person with specialized knowledge whom the rest of the group needs.

WHAT TO WATCH OUT FOR

Taking too much time. This technique can drag on, depending on the topic and readings. But when planned well the whole exercise takes two hours with participants feeling they have learned a lot and have been part of some worthwhile discussions.

Didacticism. The second round can become overly didactic, with experts assuming they need to lecture, so you will need to remind them to share a few simple points and then rely on questions to open up discussion.

Pointlessness. This should not be a series of teach-ins just to change the pace of a meeting, class, or workshop. It should always be linked to increasing needed knowledge and skill and, when appropriate, to preparing groups to take informed actions.

QUESTIONS THAT FIT THIS PROTOCOL

Any question that is complex enough to be broken down into subtopics fits well, such as the following:

- "How is this data interpreted from theoretical perspectives 1, 2, and 3?"
- "How do we integrate this priority into the different aspects of our mission?"
- "What does critical thinking look like in these different disciplines?"
- "How do we improve writing across the curriculum?"
- "What are the components of effective practice?"

CHAPTER 39

Titling the Text

This exercise promotes peoples' serious engagement with a piece of writing. Instead of having to summarize key ideas they suggest titles for the text (which is left deliberately untitled).

PURPOSES

· To give people practice in reading, analyzing, and discussing a text very closely
· To identify the main ideas in a text and to justify their selection

HOW IT WORKS

· Participants are given a short untitled article of about seven hundred words—roughly the length of a typical op-ed column—to read on their own.

- Individually they make a few notes about the main idea of the article and think about a possible title for the article.
- In groups of five or six, each member proposes a title and describes how this reflects the main idea covered.
- The group chooses a single title that best reflects the article's main idea. Creative mixing and matching occurs as members incorporate elements of different titles.
- Each group presents its title and reasons for choosing it to the gathering.
- The whole group discusses strengths and weaknesses of the various titles and then selects the one that best fits the article.

WHERE AND WHEN IT WORKS WELL

This can work just about anywhere to get people talking about the key ideas embedded in a text. The text can be anything from a mission statement or executive summary to an excerpt from a required reading.

Academic settings. Identifying the main idea and offering a relevant title is a common item on standardized assessments in high school and college.

Branding start-up projects. Organizations and communities moving in a new direction or developing a new program need to communicate to intended audiences and users what the new initiative stands for. Titling a chunk of text that describes a new program's goals can sometimes produce a succinct amalgamation that immediately communicates the new program's essence.

In retreats. In organizational or community retreats, this technique can help clarify the commitment or purpose that unites a group of people. Titling a mission statement or end-of-year summary of accomplishments helps reaffirm fundamental beliefs.

WHAT USERS APPRECIATE

It unleashes creativity. This activity feels like a form of brainstorming and free-associating that appeals to many right-brain learners.

It focuses thinking. This seems relatively simple but is often quite hard. People report enjoying the challenge of talking this through with colleagues.

WHAT TO WATCH OUT FOR

Uninformed choices. For creative types it's tempting to generate smart titles that don't communicate the main idea of the text.

Not giving reasons. Groups sometimes shortchange the process by generating titles without giving reasons. You need to remind participants that sharing the explanations for their choice of title is crucial. Allow enough time for this.

Neglecting to model the process. Outside academe this might be an unfamiliar exercise, so you might want to project a short passage on a screen and then offer some possible titles based on your understanding of the main idea.

QUESTIONS THAT FIT THIS PROTOCOL

The question is the same regardless of the text used: "What is the main idea in this reading and what title most effectively captures this main idea?"

CHAPTER 40

Critical Debate

A debate is not a discussion. In debate you try to convince some-one your position is correct and listen to another's point of view only to discover its weak points in order to refute what he or she is saying; so it may seem strange that this technique is included in our book. However, our formulation of *Critical Debate* requires someone to engage seriously with a viewpoint or perspective he or she has previously dismissed as irrelevant or inaccurate. Both of us regard this as integral to discussion.

PURPOSES

- To encourage people to consider views previously dismissed as irrelevant or inaccurate

· To create a relatively nonthreatening environment in which participants are required to critique their own deeply held viewpoints

HOW IT WORKS

· Facilitators find a contentious issue on which opinion is divided among participants and frame the issue as a debate motion.
· They ask for a show of hands of people to volunteer to work on two teams: one that prepares arguments to support the motion and one that drafts arguments opposing it.
· When the teams are settled you announce that the team that volunteered to draft arguments to support the motion will now comprise the team to draft arguments opposing it. Similarly, the team that volunteered to oppose the motion is now the one developing arguments to support it.
· Teams are told they are not expected to alter their personal views or believe anything they say in the debate. For thirty minutes they will pretend to occupy a position opposite to their real one.
· Conduct the debate. Each team works on developing its arguments for fifteen minutes then chooses one person to present it. Each representative has five minutes to make his or her case in the debate. After initial presentations the teams reconvene to draft rebuttal arguments and choose a different person to present these. The rebuttals also take five minutes for each team to present.
· The whole group debriefs about how people felt arguing against positions they were committed to. What new ways of

thinking about the issue opened up? Did new understandings emerge? Did anyone change his or her position on the issue? Which assumptions were confirmed and which challenged by this experience?

WHEN AND WHERE IT WORKS WELL

When groups are divided. This can be an effective way of building communication in groups split on a divisive issue.

If a group is myopic. When group members can't see past their own viewpoint, this helps jerk them out of their perceptual ruts.

Whenever perspective taking is needed. If organizational or community members can't appreciate other people's concerns, *Critical Debate* temporarily increases their capacity for empathic understanding of a contrary viewpoint.

To identify organizational and individual blind spots. Participating in this activity can help groups become aware of the viewpoints they habitually ignore.

WHAT USERS APPRECIATE

The purposeful artificiality of the exercise. People know they are playing at taking an opposite view and they aren't expected to change how they think.

Its theatricality. Participants use outlandish gestures or exaggerated vocal emphasis as they argue their position in the debate.

The competition. People enjoy competing against an opposite team. They cheer their side, give a thumbs down sign to their opponents, and so on.

WHAT TO WATCH OUT FOR

You can only do this once. Try it again and people will volunteer to be on the team they don't want to join knowing that you will switch the teams.

You must be trusted. Do this too soon in your time with a group and they will feel manipulated and betrayed. If this happens nobody will take it seriously.

QUESTIONS SUITED TO THIS TECHNIQUE

We have used this when people disagree on tactics within social movements ("Should we work with this organizational structure to secure change or dissociate from it entirely?") or when a difference exists on what constitutes ethical practice ("Decisions only have democratic legitimacy if they are supported by a majority").

CHAPTER 41

Single Word Sum-Ups

This gets everyone participating in discussion without making extended comments. It also tests for understanding and demonstrates the possibility of multiple interpretations.

PURPOSES

- To express an idea or make a point concisely
- To give everyone a chance to speak briefly
- To identify patterns and themes of summary words and dig deeper into these

- To use selected summary words to start subsequent conversation

HOW IT WORKS

- A presentation, video, or discussion on a concept, theory, idea, or technique takes place for ten to fifteen minutes.
- Each member then writes down on a notecard the single word he or she thinks best sums up the content explored so far.
- The large group forms a circle and each person, in turn and without interruption, reads his or her word.
- A recorder writes these words on a newsprint wall or board. The facilitator can also record these electronically to create a word cloud.
- Once all the words are spoken and written down, everyone in the group comes to the newsprint or board. They are given a marker to underline, emphasize, connect, or otherwise indicate (including with written comments) discernible patterns, themes, linkages, and opposing viewpoints.
- Members then return to their seats and continue a whole-group discussion of the content using the data from the newsprint as a springboard for their comments.

WHERE AND WHEN IT WORKS WELL

When group process has become sluggish and routine. At the simplest level, the one-word sum-ups are always a nice change of pace.

When uneven patterns of participation are developing. This is a quick and nonthreatening way to hear from an entire group.

To stimulate new thinking about complex ideas. Providing single words and exploring relationships among these opens up new channels of communication.

When participants don't know each other. This eases people into conversation when they're unsure of what to expect from each other.

WHAT USERS APPRECIATE

Its brevity. The whole exercise, including the debriefing, can be done in fifteen to twenty minutes.

Its novelty. This shakes things up for people, so it's a good way to introduce energy into a flagging format.

Its safety for introverts and ESL speakers. Giving a single word is something that nearly everyone can do, and making newsprint connections requires no speech.

Its visual element. Similar to *Chalk Talk* (technique 2) and *Newsprint Dialogue* (technique 4), the graphic nature of this activity is a boon to visually oriented learners.

WHAT TO WATCH OUT FOR

The constraint of a single word. Sometimes it's frustrating to search for a single word that captures an idea, yet allowing more than one word prolongs the exercise, so despite the limits it imposes, one word works best.

Problems of interpretation. Sometimes it's hard to see the thinking behind a word choice. Putting the summary words on a board enables people to have the chance to connect different words, underscore concepts that appear repeatedly, or use inequality symbols and lightning bolts to suggest conflicts.

Straying from the words. In the culminating whole-group discussion it's easy for people to neglect their exact words, so facilitators will need to keep people focusing on these.

The misplaced quest for profundity. Sometimes people think that because they are confined to only one word, it should be weighty, allegorical, or allusive. Although we encourage creativity, we don't want people to be pressured to come up with an astoundingly profound word.

QUESTIONS THAT FIT THIS PROTOCOL

· "What single word best sums up for you what you have just heard and seen?"
· "How are the single words that people came up with related to each other, similar to each other, or even, in some cases, opposed to each other?"
· "What recurring themes or patterns do you discern between and across the words?"

CHAPTER 42

Setting Ground Rules

Many discussions go awry simply because no attempt has been made to develop ground rules for discussion. This technique gets everyone involved in doing this.

PURPOSES
· To help discussants identify the specific behaviors that are likely to contribute to more fruitful conversations
· To give discussants practice in enacting these behaviors in an actual conversation

HOW IT WORKS

- People begin by individually and silently writing down recollections of their best and worst discussion experiences. They are told to note specifically and concretely what features made discussions so satisfying or frustrating.
- People gather in small groups of four to six members and each person shares his or her notes.
- Groups then brainstorm all the specific things that people do to make discussions go well. These often include behaviors such as people listening closely, keeping one's own comments brief, staying on topic, asking good questions, everybody speaking, and so on.
- Groups also share things people do in discussions that are frustrating. These are often the mirror image of the first set of behaviors, for example, people not listening, constantly interrupting, going off track, a few people dominating, and so on.
- Small groups then list on newsprint all the features of enjoyable discussions.
- The facilitator asks groups to convert the most frequently mentioned features to specific behaviors that should be encouraged. For example, if people like discussions in which nobody dominates they might suggest that after speaking people should wait until at least three others have contributed something (technique 48, *The Three-Person Rule*).
- Groups list on newsprint the behaviors they've identified.
- A brief discussion then takes place addressing a question such as "What do we want to accomplish today?" with members attempting to carry out chosen behaviors.

WHERE AND WHEN IT WORKS WELL

With groups just starting their deliberations. This is one of the first things new groups should do.

In academic settings. Because discussion is frequently used in higher education, this exercise works well to create a culture of discussion.

In decision-making teams. This works well with teams that pride themselves on making good decisions, such as trying out something to improve the process.

People with little experience of discussion. Students transitioning to college, community groups engaged in neighborhood activism, and members of institutions who are relaxing their decision-making procedures all find this useful.

WHAT USERS APPRECIATE

Having their experiences acknowledged. Because the ground rules spring out of people's experiences, they feel they're being treated respectfully.

Being an active contributor to determining group process. When you're involved in a process for developing ground rules, it's easier to remember and follow them.

Its concreteness. People find it helpful to have very specific rules they can practice in future discussions.

WHAT TO WATCH OUT FOR

Timing going astray. The reflections about best and worst discussions must be no more than ten minutes; otherwise, groups delay in getting to the important work of identifying concrete behaviors.

Not being concrete enough. Groups need to be pushed to get specific and concrete about these behaviors. Facilitators can help by providing examples of specific behaviors that typically contribute to productive discussions and pressing participants to name others.

QUESTIONS THAT FIT THIS PROTOCOL

This technique focuses on developing the capacity to participate in discussions of external questions, so there are no suggestions for specific topics given here other than "What's the best and the worst discussions you ever been a part of?"

CHAPTER 43

Canvassing for Common Ground

During discussions about highly controversial and contentious issues it's easy to lock into areas of disagreement. This activity focuses on identifying areas of agreement that can become the beginning points for more constructive exploration.

PURPOSES

- To help people challenge their assumptions about those holding a contrary position (for example that opponents are uninformed, dumb, inhumane, unethical, etc.)

- To practice perspective taking—seeing, however temporarily, the logic of another's viewpoint
- To stop contentious discussions moving straight to one-sided advocacy of entrenched positions
- To identify areas of agreement to keep contentious discussions going

HOW IT WORKS

- The facilitator states a strong position on a controversial issue, for example, "The United States is the greatest country in the world," "The United States has committed genocide against its indigenous population," "Higher education should be free for everyone," "Federal income taxes should be increased," "Taxes should be abolished," "Affirmative action is ineffective and unfair and should be discontinued," "Racism is endemic in this country."
- In small groups of five or six, participants write down on newsprint all relevant evidence and arguments that support or challenge the statement. At this stage there is no agreement on or discussion of the points.
- Regarding the statement "The United States is the greatest country in the world," people might write "Great countries are prosperous," "Great countries are just," "Great countries have little or no hunger," "Great countries make a special effort to care for their children," "Great countries have a thriving education system," "Great countries have responsibility for humanity outside their borders," "The United States has great income disparities," "The United States denies justice to too

many people," "The United States has an unusually high rate of child abuse," "People of color in the United States are disproportionately incarcerated."

· Once all points are made, members check those they agree with. Points accumulating checks can be proposed as ones that might find broad agreement.

· Groups discuss and revise points until they reach agreement or it becomes clear this is impossible. Any point securing unanimous agreement is underlined.

· Members review these one last time to ensure everyone concurs and to reinforce the sense of strong agreement that has emerged.

· Groups are now free to discuss anything, including revising areas of strong disagreement.

· They can institute additional agreements to see if new common ground has emerged.

· The whole group assembles to share points of agreement and to consider whether or not the search for common ground reduced the usual level of contentiousness.

WHERE AND WHEN IT WORKS WELL

With institutions that operate by consensus. Quaker communities and institutions usually find this familiar and congenial.

Organizations, communities, and groups struggling with conflict. Divided groups needing to act on contentious issues can use this to build agreement.

When seeking to recover from a divisive event or major change. Organizations, communities, and groups that have recently had to deal with crises—hate crimes on campus, downsizing and layoffs, a changed mission statement, a new strategic plan—can benefit from reappraising what still are areas of common agreement.

WHAT USERS APPRECIATE

The focus on areas of agreement. This is appealing and motivating for those tired of conflict.

How it alleviates contentiousness. Discussion that ensues after identifying areas of agreement tends to be less hobbled by conflict and acrimony.

WHAT TO WATCH OUT FOR

Generating points about a statement. Sometimes what facilitators view as contentious statements are seen as unremarkable. Participants then have a hard time generating arguments or evidence for and against the statement. An alternative is for conveners to write out points beforehand so groups can begin naming areas of agreement without delay.

Routinized consensus. Organizational and community cultures often interpret being a good team player as agreeing with or supporting others. Even when disagreement exists it is easier to say "Uh huh," nod, or just stay quiet. So test the waters ahead of time to make sure your statements are especially contentious to the group you're working with. Or use statements that are so controversial that some disagreement is inevitable.

212

Unbridgeable positions. Sometimes issues are so divisive—abortion immediately comes to mind—that a search for common ground proves impossible. If this is so, this exercise is unlikely to work.

QUESTIONS THAT FIT THIS PROTOCOL

The basis for discussion is strong, contested, controversial statements such as the ones noted in the "How It Works" section.

CHAPTER 44

Dramatizing Discussion

We draw on elements of improv theater (McKnight & Scruggs, 2008) and theater of the oppressed (Boal, 2008) for this technique. Groups respond to a question or problem by staging a short skit whose progress can be interrupted or outcome altered through the spontaneous intervention of audience members.

PURPOSES

· To unleash a group's creative energy when considering a topic or question
· To introduce an element of play into organizational routines

- To deepen understanding of a topic or question by exploring it from new and unfamiliar perspectives
- To connect to participants who learn best through movement and drama
- To help groups explore highly contentious or emotional issues
- To gain experience in imagining more desirable or socially just realities

HOW IT WORKS

- Small groups of six to eight members are given thirty minutes to discuss a question or analyze a text.
- Each group then spends another thirty minutes creating a brief skit that it believes captures the content, agreements, and disagreements of the discussion.
- Each skit is then presented to the large group.
- Any members of the large group may interrupt the skit at any time as new characters who introduce new plot elements or take skits in new directions.
- The group originating the skit can choose to follow the lead of the interrupter or continue its skit according to its initial plan.
- After all skits are presented, participants discuss how they captured the issues discussed in groups and any new insights raised.

WHERE AND WHEN IT WORKS WELL

When institutional routines have become stale. Groups that meet regularly often benefit from exercises that infuse their interactions with new energy. This technique can be a lot of fun and unleash group members' creativity.

216

With creative arts organizations. Not surprisingly this technique often works well with groups sharing a creative or artistic orientation, such as a community theatre, community arts organization, or museum.

WHAT USERS APPRECIATE

It helps groups claim empowerment. Instead of just talking about how things might be different, dramatizing discussion involves people using their minds and bodies to enact a different future. This builds momentum for change and provides an empowering glimpse into how a constraining situation can be altered.

The enlivening novelty. *Dramatizing Discussion* is utterly new for most people and its novelty is energizing and engaging.

It helps to see the world in a whole new way. People sometimes have a transformative experience that suggests an alternative way of viewing an issue.

WHAT TO WATCH OUT FOR

Risk. This is clearly one of the riskier techniques in this book. There is no guarantee that it will lead to powerful learning, and because it does involve a big investment of time, it may end up feeling like a waste to those participating. However, given how much creative energy is likely to be unleashed and how many new, fresh perspectives may emerge, it could be well worth that risk.

Untrained facilitators. Although improvising is something people do in everyday life, and particularly in conversations, converting this improvisational instinct into constructing a meaningful skit is a stretch for most of us. Dramatizing discussion greatly benefits from someone with improv training or, in the absence of that, native chutzpah!

Getting stuck. Groups sometimes get stuck at the halfway point when they have to develop a skit. It may be helpful for you to reconvene the whole workshop or class and take a few minutes to brainstorm suggestions for specific skits.

Bad timing. Don't do this in a workshop with limited time and don't do this if a group is in the early stages of its life together. The performance anxiety typically will overwhelm most people.

Intervention stress. The option to interrupt skits is exciting for some but a threat for those already feeling uneasy. Facilitators might need to model this by adding suggestions or providing new information to bring about more socially just outcomes.

Derailment. Sometimes an interruption threatens to take the skit completely off track. Remind groups that they don't have to follow a spontaneous lead.

QUESTIONS THAT FIT THIS PROTOCOL

· "What would it mean to act compassionately in our organization?"
· "What is the most controversial aspect of this text?"
· "How do we stop dissent being silenced in our community?"
· "What are the main points this text is trying to convey?"
· "How do we respond constructively when we commit a micro-aggression?"

CHAPTER 45

Deliberative Polling

Drawing on the work of James Fishkin (2009) and the Kettering Foundation's *National Issues Forum* (Melville, Willingham, & Dedrick, 2005), polling is used to prep people for a discussion and to explore how it has informed their thinking once it's concluded.

PURPOSES

- To promote deep and informed discussion about an important public policy issue
- To explore viewpoints on the issue that participants do not know well

- To gain practice in taking a stance on issues and giving reasons for that stance
- To understand the dynamics of people changing their minds in discussion

HOW IT WORKS

- Participants are polled about their initial thinking on an issue of local or national importance.
- They are then assigned briefing materials that present them with three or four clearly differentiated positions on the issue.
- They study these materials, noting areas of confusion and jotting down questions that these materials raise.
- Participants then gather for a rather lengthy discussion (up to two hours) that begins by generating ground rules governing conduct during the discussion.
- The moderator then summarizes the various positions on the issue or plays a short video that lays out the different perspectives.
- He or she then leads people through a discussion in which equal time is granted to examine assumptions, ask questions, identify areas of confusion, and share relevant experiences for each position.
- The moderator asks participants to direct their comments to each other (not to the moderator) and to ask questions that help participants articulate their assumptions and explain their reasons.
- Once all positions have been discussed, participants share what they have learned and how or whether they changed their minds as a result of the discussion.

- An exit poll is taken to assess how people have been swayed by the conversation.

WHERE AND WHEN IT WORKS WELL

Community forums. This works well in community forums in which there is shared interest in a broad public policy issue affecting a lot of people. People who are invested in the issue are more willing to take time to engage fully with the arguments and claims for various positions and to deliberate thoughtfully about desirable options.

Academic settings. *Deliberative Polling* can be a great way to investigate a topic that has three or four distinct theoretical traditions informing its study, three or four different analytical frameworks, or ethical issues that have several possible responses.

When time is not an issue. This process takes at least half a day. People have to study the position briefings, establish ground rules, and engage in a rather lengthy and intense discussion of the different positions, so only do this if there is time to do it justice.

WHAT USERS APPRECIATE

It develops critical thinking. This requires people to examine their assumptions, provide convincing evidence, and articulate reasons—all important aspects of critical thinking.

It affirms the value of informed opinions. Whether people change their minds is less relevant than whether they develop opinions informed by data and evidence.

Understanding opposing views. When people learn about contradictory viewpoints, this can help in locating areas of common ground.

221

WHAT TO WATCH OUT FOR

Fatigue. This is a lengthy process that can be trying for some participants.

Sloppy, incomplete briefing materials. For this to work well, the briefing materials on the positions must be factually accurate, clearly written, and concisely expressed. Compiling such briefing materials takes time.

Facilitator bias. Moderators must remain neutral and not implicitly support any particular position. Their job is to help people educate one another about unfamiliar and less-favored positions.

Shortchanging the final discussion. It's important to hear at the end of the discussion about what people have learned and whether their minds have been changed in any way. Make sure to leave time for this final dialogue.

QUESTIONS THAT FIT THIS PROTOCOL

Examples of policy questions could be the following:

- "What tax policies are fair and not overly burdensome, yet are sufficient to finance the nation's top priorities?"
- "What does health care in a democracy look like?"
- "How can we address the stubbornly high unemployment rate?"
- "How can a community improve mediocre public school systems?"
- "What's a just way of dealing with immigration into the US?"

CHAPTER 46

Participatory Decision Making

David Graeber's *Democracy Project* (2013) is based on the ideas that everyone affected by a decision should have an equal chance to influence it and that no one should be bound by something he or she cannot accept. This technique puts these ideas into practice.

PURPOSES

· To develop a deeper, more appreciative understanding of reaching consensus
· To strive to reach a decision in which everyone involved feels his or her viewpoint and concerns have been heard and responded to

- To practice developing the ground rules of consensus decision making

HOW IT WORKS

- The facilitator starts by establishing some basic principles that parallel Graeber's (2013) ideas for moving toward consensus:

  Principle 1: Anyone who wants to weigh in with a point of view about a proposal or course of action must have the opportunity to be heard.

  Principle 2: Anyone with objections or concerns about a proposal should have a legitimate chance to influence the outcome in some way.

  Principle 3: Anyone who wishes to veto or block a proposal because it violates a vital principle should have his or her concerns used to reformulate the proposal.

  Principle 4: No one should be required to go along with a proposal he or she regards as unacceptable.

- Someone proposes a particular decision or course of action that he or she feels will address a problem.
- Clarifying questions are invited to ensure everyone understands the proposal.
- Facilitators ask participants to register concerns including (1) friendly amendments, (2) temperature checks to capture a group's attitude about a specific proposal, and (3) suggestions for revision such as combining it with other proposals or eliminating it altogether.
- Facilitators invite "stand-asides"—objections that are not so strong as to block the proposal but that offer clues about some of its possible weaknesses.

- They then ask for "blocks"—something that can stop a proposal in its tracks or lead to further discussion and possible compromise. If there are no blocks and stand-asides are minimal, that may be sufficient to regard it as acceptable.
- A vote may also be taken in which the vote of a super-majority—say 70 percent of the whole—passes the proposal. At the height of the Occupy Movement, this figure was raised to 90 percent of the whole when such votes were found necessary or expedient.

AN ABRIDGED VERSION

It is also possible to try out this process in a greatly abridged form:

- In decision-making discussions facilitators propose a rule that no comment can be made at any time that does not explicitly refer back to and build on a previous speaker's comment.
- Facilitators take clarifying questions about the issue to be addressed.
- Concerns are raised along with possible moves to revise or even eliminate the proposal.
- The facilitator asks for stand-asides.
- The facilitator asks for blocks.
- The facilitator asks everyone to show his or her level of support—five fingers for strong support, one finger for stand-aside, fist for block.
- A decision is made based on a sense of the whole or a formal vote requiring a 70 percent super-majority.
- Participants debrief the experience of making decisions by a consensus process.

WHERE AND WHEN IT WORKS WELL

Community groups. In grassroots groups or town hall meetings this is less legalistic than, say, Robert's Rules of Order.

In hierarchical organizational and academic settings. This is often an eye-opener for those who think working for consensus invites chaos. They are surprised by its structure and ability to accommodate a wide range of differing opinions.

WHAT USERS APPRECIATE

Being clear and inclusive. People appreciate the emphasis on carefully framing, refining, and vetting proposals before they are brought to a vote.

Honoring every voice. This enables every person to contribute to decision making but also acknowledges objections (stand-asides and blocks) even while working to reach wide agreement.

WHAT TO WATCH OUT FOR

Make and good ground rule proposal. The first step in making a consensus process real is to try out a proposal that will honestly affect how people interact in a meaningful discussion. One might be that no one can speak in a meeting or discussion unless he or she refers to and builds on a previous speaker's comment. Others could be that no contribution exceeds one minute or that every speaker contributes at least once during each workshop or class session.

Frivolous blocks. Early on people may attempt a block because they dislike some aspect of a proposal. This should be allowed to go forward to see how the group grapples with this challenge, but watch out for blocks being used indiscriminately anytime someone has a minor objection. These should be reserved only for situations in which there is a very strong objection to the proposal.

QUESTIONS THAT FIT THIS PROTOCOL

This is a technique for ensuring that the highest number of people participate in making a decision, so any question a community wishes to resolve is appropriate.

CHAPTER 47

Mutual Invitation

Developed by Episcopalian priest Eric Law, *Mutual Invitation* is a technique designed to promote egalitarian group talk that works best in smaller groups in which people already know something about each other's skills, knowledge, and experience.

PURPOSES

· To create an opportunity for everyone in a group to contribute to a discussion
· To put the control of group process in the group's hands
· To ground the discussion in what most concerns and interests group members

HOW IT WORKS

- Facilitators begin by giving their views on a topic or question.
- The facilitator then chooses the next person to share whatever she or he wishes to. This person is allowed plenty of time to think about what to say and should not feel compelled to spring into speech.
- After the second speaker has finished, he or she then chooses who is to speak next.
- When someone is invited to speak, that person can pass, but he or she still chooses the next speaker.
- The process continues until everyone has had the chance to speak.
- Those who passed earlier in the discussion are invited to say whatever they wish to about the topic.
- The process then moves into open discussion.

WHERE AND WHEN IT WORKS WELL

In congregations. Originally developed for congregational use, this exercise is widely used in Bible study or congregational decision making.

In long-standing groups. Because people know each other well, they are well placed to decide whom to call on next based on their expertise and experience.

With groups that have developed an exclusionary pecking order. This ensures that everyone participates, with a person's potential to enrich the conversation determining decisions about who will speak next, not positional authority.

WHAT USERS APPRECIATE

Democratic process. The emphasis is on everybody getting the same chance to contribute.

Exercising control. Members are in total control of the order of contributions and the direction of the discussion.

Being recognized. Receiving a direct request to speak is often extremely affirming, particularly when the reasons for that choice are provided (for example, "I'd like to hear from John now because of his experience with marginalized groups").

WHAT TO WATCH OUT FOR

Running out of time. Unless the facilitator keeps track of time, some members will speak for too long. Eric Law suggests letting people know in advance roughly how long they should speak.

Feeling unappreciated. Sometimes those who are chosen to speak toward the end of the process feel as if they're back in the school or neighborhood playground being the last to be called on to join pick-up teams.

Performance anxiety. Hearing well-constructed contributions as you're waiting for your turn to be called can build tension.

The stress of being called on to speak next. When the invitation to speak finally comes, it can feel as if you're being jumped on, particularly if you don't feel you have anything relevant to say.

Being unable to contribute something pertinent in the moment. As people hear the conversation progress, there are many times they want to join in but are not allowed because they have not been chosen to speak.

Unfamiliarity. If group members know little about each other they have no real information to inform decisions about who should be chosen next.

QUESTIONS SUITED TO THIS TECHNIQUE

This works best in smaller-sized groups (eight to twelve) in which everyone brings relevant experience to the topic at hand. Examples might be as follows:

- "How do we want to accomplish this task?"
- "What should our response be to this situation?"
- "How can we improve how our community arrives at decisions?"
- "What have we missed in our reaction to this problem over the past year?"
- "What do we do about this criticism leveled at our organization?"

CHAPTER 48

The Three-Person Rule

This is an easy rule for participants to remember in large-group discussions.

PURPOSES

- To stop a small minority from monopolizing a large-group discussion
- To create opportunities for multiple people to contribute
- To socialize people into listening to several people before making a follow-up comment

HOW IT WORKS

- The facilitator opens a large-group discussion by proposing a ground rule to ensure that as many voices as possible are heard: once someone has contributed something to the discussion he or she should not contribute again until at least three other people have spoken.
- This rule should *not* be in effect, however, if someone asks a speaker to clarify, explain, or expand on a contribution she or he has just made.
- As the discussion proceeds, facilitators monitor how the rule is being followed and, when necessary, step in to ask that it be observed.

WHERE AND WHEN IT WORKS WELL

With large groups. This is best suited to larger-group discussion.
To break an established pecking order. If a group has already established a predictable pattern of contributions, *The Three-Person Rule* can help disrupt this pattern to open up the process to a wider range of views.
To slow down the tendency to rush to judgment. This technique tends to introduce longer deliberative periods of silence that stop groups from rushing to premature conclusions or decisions driven by the most verbose.

WHAT USERS APPRECIATE

Removing intimidation. Those who feel intimidated by two or three powerful voices value the democratizing of the conversation.

Its simplicity. Facilitators and participants tell us they like the simplicity of the rule and how easy it is to understand and follow. **Time to process.** Introverts and those who need more time to process information appreciate the extended time they enjoy when this rule is followed.

WHAT TO WATCH OUT FOR

People forgetting the rule. In this case you step in and remind them of it.

Awkward silences. Because a few confident and articulate extroverts no longer control group deliberations, there will be many more gaps in the discussion. You need to remind people that this is normal and that silent thinking and processing is crucial for informed discussion.

People feeling silenced. Extraverts sometimes feel this rule silences them. If this happens you need to rejustify why the rule is in place.

QUESTIONS SUITED TO THIS ACTIVITY

The Three-Person Rule can be adapted for discussion that happens in response to any kind of question posed.

CHAPTER 49

Conversational Roles

People unused to open discussion often find it difficult to participate and cede the floor to more experienced group members or extroverts. By assigning conversational roles, people are given specific guidance and direction on how to participate. Surprisingly (at least for the two of us), many who are unused to discussion experience this as helpful. Having a specific role to play provides a reassuring focus.

PURPOSES
· To create diverse ways of engaging in discussion
· To prevent a discussion from focusing on only one topic

- To provide reassuring guidance on how to participate in discussion for those unused to this activity
- To make sure the discussion stays fresh

HOW IT WORKS

- Facilitators prepare a number of discussion roles on 3' × 5' cards, together with a brief description of how each role is played.
- These cards are placed face down into a bowl, hat, or box and participants choose one at random. They look at their role and its description without showing their card to anyone.
- Facilitators tell people that in the upcoming discussion they should try to play their particular role whenever possible. However, they explain that participating in the discussion in ways that don't conform to the role is also welcome.
- Common roles people are asked to play are the following:
  - *Problem poser.* Start the discussion off by describing how the problem, question, or issue relates to your experience or what part of the topic you think is the most important to address.
  - *Devil's advocate or dissenter.* Listen carefully for any emerging consensus. When you hear this, try to formulate and express a contrary view.
  - *Umpire.* Listen for judgmental comments that sound offensive, insulting, and demeaning and bring these to people's attention.
  - *Connector.* Do your best to show how participants' contributions are connected to each other.
  - *Appreciator.* Show how you find another's ideas interesting or useful.

- *Speculator.* Try to introduce new ideas, new interpretations, and possible lines of inquiry into the group, for example, "I wonder what would happen if... ?" "I wonder what [major theorist] would say about... ?"
- *Illustrator.* Provide as many examples as you can of points that illustrate the arguments others are making.
- *Active listener.* Try to paraphrase others' contributions to the conversation ("So what I hear you saying is... " "If I understand you correctly you're suggesting that... ") or provide illustrations that extend someone's contribution.
- *Underscorer.* Emphasize the relevance, accuracy, or resonance of another person's comments and explain why these are so pertinent.
- *Evidential assessor.* Listen for comments that generalize or make unsupported assertions. Ask for the evidence that supports the assertions expressed.
- *Questioner.* When possible try to pose questions that lead to a deeper discussion, for example, "Can you give an example of that?" "What would that look like?" "How does your point connect to theory A?"
- At the end of the discussion people share the roles they were asked to play and talk about the challenge of doing this.

WHERE AND WHEN IT WORKS WELL

Academic settings. Incoming freshman often appreciate the guidance and structure of playing a specific role as an introduction to college-level discussion.

If a group's culture is too competitive or adversarial. If group members see being effective in discussion as arguing for their viewpoint as strongly as possible, taking on a connector, appreciator, active listener, or underscorer role can help broaden their range of discussion behaviors.

When you wish to alter habitual participation patterns. When people are assigned different roles it helps break up the usual way that members interact with one another.

WHAT USERS APPRECIATE

Structure. Being given a role to play provides the security of knowing what is expected of you during a discussion.

Variety. The different roles tend to keep the discussion more interesting and stop it from running out of steam too soon.

WHAT TO WATCH OUT FOR

Focusing too much on a role. Sometimes people become so preoccupied with playing a role that it stops them from participating in the discussion. It's important to emphasize that playing the role should not prevent anyone from making other kinds of contributions.

Complexity. Some of the roles are more demanding than others. Being devil's advocate, evidential assessor, or umpire, for example, requires more skill than being an appreciator or connector. Sometimes it helps if you assign the more complex roles to people whom you think can handle these so the less-skilled participants can see what they look like.

Roles being played inexpertly. Without some detailed demonstration of what playing these roles looks like, people can blunder in and cause more harm than good. For example, an umpire can point out an infraction against group ground rules in a way that's highly personal and judgmental. To show what each of these roles look like, you as facilitator can model playing them in meetings and discussions: "now I'm going to play the role of devil's advocate" or "for the next five minutes I'm going to be an evidential assessor."

QUESTIONS THAT SUIT THIS PROTOCOL

The questions that are being asked will determine many of the roles being played. For example, if your question is one designed to challenge groupthink or organizational norms, then the devil's advocate or dissenter, speculator, and evidential assessor roles become more important. If the question is designed to assess participants' understanding of complex material, then the illustrator and questioner roles are crucial.

CHAPTER 50

Facilitator Summary

As a facilitator you want to encourage as much free-flowing discussion as possible. But as it proceeds, you occasionally hear contributions that you think are uninformed, omit important data, or display a fundamental misunderstanding of what's being talked about. What to do? If a previously taciturn group is finally starting to catch conversational fire the last thing you want to do is douse the flames by correcting people who are speaking up for the first time. In such situations we use the *Facilitator Summary*, a time at the end of the session reserved for us to make some overall comments. Here we owe a debt to Ira Shor's (1997) notion of dialogic lecturing: making observations that are grounded in earlier student discussion.

PURPOSES

· To enable facilitators time to correct misunderstandings and factual errors expressed during a discussion
· To enable facilitators to bring omitted perspectives, ignored voices, and unacknowledged data to the attention of discussants
· To provide an opportunity for discussion conveners to add their viewpoints to the mix
· To create an opportunity for facilitators to comment on the process of the discussion: what went well, what major questions and issues emerged, how things might be improved next time, and questions to consider

HOW IT WORKS

· At the start of a discussion facilitators explain to the group members that their role will be restricted to asking questions, making sure everyone has a chance to speak, and trying to keep the discussion on topic.
· They say they will be listening carefully to what's being said and that if misstatements, errors, omissions, and misunderstandings are expressed they will make a note to bring these to everyone's attention at the end of the session. They explain they will be doing this is because their main task is to keep the discussion flowing, not to keep interrupting.
· About ten minutes before time is up the facilitator intervenes to give a summary of what's been missed, misinterpreted, and misstated as well as commenting on the group's process.

WHEN AND WHERE IT WORKS WELL

Academic settings. This is very appropriate for discussions in which students are struggling to interpret and apply new material.
Problem-solving meetings. When people are in a brainstorming phase, tossing out multiple solutions and interpretations, they can't afford to be interrupted.
Training workshops. This works well when people are trying to understand what new legislation means for their work or are struggling to apply a mandatory new technique.
When trust has not yet developed. The summary is best suited to groups in which facilitators judge that intervening to correct a comment will silence people permanently. It becomes less necessary as trust builds.

WHAT USERS APPRECIATE

Avoiding public shaming. Those who have been in error appreciate the fact that they have not been called out and publicly humiliated by the leader.
Respecting truth. Those who know a contribution is wrong or reflects a fundamental misunderstanding are glad to see the instructor point this out.
Facilitator disclosure. Those who have been wondering what you are thinking are able to hear your judgments and perspectives.

WHAT TO WATCH OUT FOR

Blatant errors. Sometimes people are so far off that you have to intervene. This would be the case if someone claimed as a key fact or a central truth something you knew to be wrong or if a concept or theory was explained in a way that contradicted its true meaning. Having discussion based on a central misunderstanding isn't helpful.

Comments out of context. Sometimes the comments you want to make at the end of a session are so removed from the context in which the original points were made that it is difficult to recall what was actually said and why it was important.

The problem of recollection. Just trying to remember all the things you had hoped to point out at the end of a session can be a challenge for any facilitator.

QUESTIONS THAT FIT THIS PROTOCOL

This is not a protocol to develop questions.

BIBLIOGRAPHY

Alinsky, S. *Rules for Radicals: A Pragmatic Primer for Realistic Radicals.* New York: Vintage Books, 1971.

Baptiste, I. "Beyond Reason and Personal Integrity: Toward a Pedagogy of Coercive Restraint." *Canadian Journal for the Study of Adult Education,* 2000, Volume 14, No. 1, 27–50.

Bligh, D. A. *What's the Use of Lectures?* San Francisco: Jossey-Bass, 2000.

Boal, A. *Games for Actors and Non-Actors* (2nd Edition). New York: Routledge, 2008.

Bohm, D. *On Dialogue.* London: Routledge, 1996.

Brookfield, S. D. (Ed.). *Learning Democracy: Eduard Lindeman on Adult Education and Social Change.* Beckenham, UK: Croom Helm, 1988.

Elbow, P. *Embracing Contraries: Explorations in Teaching and Learning.* New York: Oxford University Press, 1986.

Fishkin, J. *The People Speak: Deliberative Democracy and Public Consultation.* New York: Oxford University Press, 2009.

Graeber, D. *The Democracy Project: A History, A Crisis, A Movement.* New York: Spiegel and Grau, 2013.

Habermas, J. *The Theory of Communicative Action, Volume One: Reason and the Rationalization of Society.* Boston: Beacon Press, 1984.

Law, E. *The Wolf Shall Dwell with the Lamb.* St. Louis, MO: Chalice Press, 1993.

Lyman, F. "The Responsive Classroom Discussion: The Inclusion of All Students." *Mainstreaming Digest.* College Park: University of Maryland, 1981.

McNight, K. S., and M. Scruggs. *The Second City Guide to Using Improv in the Classroom: Using Improvisation to Teach Skills and Boost Learning*. San Francisco: Jossey-Bass, 2008.

Melville, K., Willingham, T., Dedrick, J. "National Issues Forums: A Network of Communities Promoting Public Deliberation." In Gastil, J. and Levine, P. (Eds.), *The Deliberative Democracy Handbook: Strategies for Effective Civic Engagement in the 21st Century*. San Francisco: Jossey-Bass, 2005, 37–58.

Mezirow, J. *Transformative Dimensions of Adult Learning*. San Francisco: Jossey-Bass, 1991.

Palmer, P. J. *The Courage to Teach: Transforming the Inner Landscape of a Teacher's Life* (Tenth Anniversary Edition). San Francisco: Jossey-Bass, 2007.

Phillips, C. *Socrates Café: A Fresh Taste of Philosophy*. New York: W. W. Norton, 2001.

Rothstein, D., and L. Santana. *Make Just One Change: Teach Students to Ask Their Own Questions*. Cambridge, MA: Harvard Education Press, 2011.

Shor, I. *When Students Have Power: Negotiating Authority in a Critical Pedagogy*. Chicago: University of Chicago Press, 1997.

Smith, H. "The Foxfire Approach to Student and Community Interaction." In L. Shumow (Ed.), *Promising Practices for Family and Community Involvement during High School*. Charlotte, NC: Information Age Publishing, 2009.

Stevenson, B. "We Need to Talk About an Injustice." Retrieved from https://www.ted.com/talks/bryan_stevenson_we_need_to_talk_about_an_injustice/, March 2012. Video File.

Stevenson, B. *Just Mercy: A Story of Redemption and Justice*. New York: Spiegel and Grau, 2014.

Wah, L. M. *The Color of Fear*. Oakland, CA: Stir Fry Productions, 1994.

248

INDEX

254